Three Dialogues on Kn

Three Dialogues on Knowledge

Paul K. Feyerabend

Basil Blackwell

This edition first published 1991

Basil Blackwell Ltd
108 Cowley Road, Oxford, OX4 1JF, UK

Basil Blackwell, Inc.
3 Cambridge Center
Cambridge, Massachusetts 02142, USA

British Library Cataloguing in Publication Data

A CIP catalogue record for this book is available from the British Library.

Library of Congress Cataloging in Publication Data
Feyerabend, Paul K., 1924–
Three dialogues on knowledge/Paul K. Feyerabend.
p. cm.
Includes bibliographical references and index.
ISBN 0–631–17917–8:—ISBN 0–631–17918–6:
1. Knowledge, Theory of. 2. Metaphysics. 3. Ethics. I. Title.
BD161.F42 1991
121—dc20 90–1292
CIP

Typeset in 10½ on 12 pt Aster
by Graphicraft Typesetters Ltd., Hong Kong
Printed in Great Britain by T. J. Press Ltd., Padstow, Cornwall.

Contents

First Dialogue (*1990*)

First Dialogue

(The scene is a seminar at a well-known university. A shabby little room with a table and chairs. Looking out of the window one sees trees, birds, parked cars and two power shovels trying to dig a large hole. Slowly the room fills with a variety of characters, among them Arnold, a serious bespectacled student with lots of books under his arm and a contemptuous look on his face, Maureen, an attractive red-haired lady who seems a little confused, Leslie, a bum, or at least a character – possibly another student – who looks like a bum, and seems ready to leave at the drop of a hat, Donald, a nondescript individual with a notebook and a carefully sharpened pencil, Charles, a Korean student, mocking eyes behind shining spectacles, Seidenberg, an elderly gentleman with a heavy central European accent, somewhat uncomfortable in the surroundings, Lee Feng, a Chinese student, a physicist, or mathematician, to judge from the titles of the books he is putting on the table, Gaetano, shy and young, looks like somebody who might write poems, Jack, a logician with the casual habits and the precise diction of the US version of that profession, carries a large briefcase ... Enter Dr Cole, the professor of the class, about 32, a new addition to the faculty, intelligent in a narrow way, just finished a thesis on scepticism under the supervision of Donald Davidson, ready to spread knowledge as he understands it.)

Dr Cole (opens his mouth).
(First power shovel roars.)
(Second power shovel roars.)
Leslie (makes a comment and laughs; Donald seems to have understood, looks outraged).
Dr Cole (leaves to set matters right).
(Double roar of the power shovels.)
(Ten minutes later: Dr Cole returns, gesticulates towards the door, leaves; the others follow with a resigned look on their faces.)
Maureen (*walking along on the corridor, to Arnold*): Is this the class on postmodern cooking?
Leslie (*who heard her, laughs out loud*): Postmodern cooking? You can't go wrong. That's the course.
Arnold: No, it isn't. This is a seminar on epistemology!
Leslie: What's the difference? Let her stay!
Maureen: But I really would like to ...
Dr Cole (*gesturing towards another room)*: In here, please.
(*Now we have a huge room without windows, with a table and some very new but also very uncomfortable chairs.*)
Dr Cole (*sits down at the head of the table)*: I am sorry for the delay and the confusion. At last, we can now start with our seminar on epistemology ...
David and Bruce (*appear at the door)*: Is this the philosophy seminar?
Dr Cole (*slightly exasperated)*: One of them. There are others ...
David (*looking at the catalogue)*: ... I mean the one on epi ... epi ...
Bruce: Epistemology.
David: Yeah; that's the one we want.
Dr Cole (*more exasperated than before)*: I hope you know what you are doing. Please sit down. (*Sits down himself, opens his briefcase, pulls out notes and a copy of the* Theaetetus.) Well, what I wanted to say is that I thought it best to have a focus for our discussion, not just to wander around, and that is why I suggested that today we discuss Plato's dialogue *Theaetetus*.
Jack: Isn't that a little behind the times?
Dr Cole: What do you mean?
Jack: Well (*pulls a copy of the dialogue out of his briefcase*) this guy lived over two thousand years ago, he didn't know modern logic and modern science, so what can we learn from him about knowledge?

Bruce: And scientists, you think, do know what knowledge is?
Jack: They don't talk about it, they produce it.
Bruce: I don't know what sciences you have in mind but in my field, in sociology, there is an ongoing debate about the 'correct method'. On the one side we are told that there cannot be any knowledge without statistics. Others say that you have to 'get the feel' for the area you are examining, so you study individual cases in detail and write about them almost like a novelist. There just was a minor scandal about a book *The Social Transformation of American Medicine*; the author, Paul Starr, discussed some very interesting phenomena, he had evidence, but he had no numbers; influential sociologists refused to take him seriously; other equally influential sociologists defended him and criticized the way in which statistics was being used. In psychology we have behaviourists, introspectionists, neurologists, clinical psychologists ...
Jack: Well, the social sciences ...
Bruce: They are sciences, are they not?
Jack: Did you guys ever get something as simple, beautiful and successful as Newton's theory?
David: Of course not! People are more complicated than the planets! Why, your wonderful natural sciences can't even deal with the weather ...
Arthur (*has been listening at the door and now enters; to Jack*): I am sorry, I could not help overhearing. I am a historian of science. I think you have a somewhat simple idea about Newton. First of all, what you call 'simple and beautiful' is not the same thing as what you call 'successful' – at least not in Newton. 'Simple and beautiful' – that's his basic principles. 'Successful' is the way in which he applies them. Here he uses a rather incoherent collection of new assumptions, among them the assumption that God periodically interferes with the planetary system to keep it from falling apart. And Newton does philosophize. He has a number of principles about the correct way of proceeding. He lays down principles of research and he is very insistent about them. The trouble is that he violates these principles the moment he starts doing research. The same is true of many other physicists. In a way scientists don't know what they are doing ...
Jack: Yeah, when they start philosophizing. I can understand why entering this confused area they get confused themselves.

Arthur: And their research remains unaffected by their confusion?
Jack: Well, if their philosophy confuses their research, that's one more reason for keeping philosophy out of science.
Arthur: And how will you do that?
Jack: Keep as closely as possible to observations!
Arthur: What about experiments?
Jack: Of course, observations and experiments!
Arthur: Why experiments?
Jack: Because observations with the naked eye are not always trustworthy.
Arthur: How do you know that?
Jack: Other observations tell me.
Arthur: You mean – one observation tells you that you can't trust another observation? How?
Jack: You don't know? Well – put a stick into water – it looks crooked. But you know it is straight by feeling it.
Arthur: How do you know that? The feeling of straightness might be mistaken!
Jack: Sticks don't bend when put in water.
Arthur: They don't? Not if you follow observation, as you advise me to. Here (*takes a glass of water that has been standing in front of Dr Cole and puts a pencil into it*) – look!
Jack: But what about what you feel when you touch it?
Arthur: Well, to be honest, I feel cold and I am not too sure that I can judge the shape of the pencil. But assume I can – well, then all I can do, according to your suggestions, is to make a list: pencil bent when looked at while in water, pencil straight when felt while in water, pencil invisible when I close my eyes . . . and so on where 'pencil' is defined by the list.
Jack: This is absurd – there is the pencil!
Arthur: OK, you want to talk about something that has stable properties even if no-one is looking at it – you can do that; but you have to go beyond observations.
Jack: OK. I agree. But this is simple commonsense; it has nothing to do with philosophy.
Arthur: But it has! Many debates in philosophy, including the debate in the dialogue before us are precisely about this question!
Jack: Well, if that is philosophy, you can have it. For me assuming that objects are not just lists of observations but

entities with properties of their own is just commonsense – and scientists follow commonsense.
Arthur: But they don't, at least not this kind of commonsense! What we have, said Heisenberg when working on one of his early papers, are spectral lines, their frequencies, their intensities – so, let's find a schematism that tells us how these things hang together without postulating any underlying 'objects'. And then he introduced matrices, which are lists, though somewhat complicated ones.
Jack: OK – so I would say that scientists follow commonsense – unless experience tells them different. There still is no need for philosophy.
Arthur: Things are not so simple! You say 'experience' – what you mean are complicated experimental results.
Jack: Yes.
Arthur: And complicated experiments often are full of bugs, especially when we enter a new domain of research. Practical bugs – some part of the equipment doesn't work as it should – and theoretical bugs – some effects were overlooked, or calculated incorrectly.
Jack: We use computers.
Arthur: You still are not safe. Computers are programmed to make approximations and these may accumulate in a way that distorts the results. At any rate – there are lots of problems. Just think of the many attempts to find single magnetic poles or isolated quarks. Some people found them, others didn't, still others found things in between . . .
Jack: What has that got to do with philosophy?
Arthur: I'll tell you in a minute! At any rate – do you agree that it would be unwise to assume that all the experiments in a new domain will at once give the same result?
Jack (*doubtful*): Yeees?
Arthur: So, a good theory, an excellent theory may be in trouble because of that phenomenon. And by a 'good' theory I mean a theory that agrees with all flawless experiments. And as it occasionally takes years, even centuries to iron out the bugs, we need a way of keeping theories alive despite the fact that they clash with the evidence.
Jack: Centuries?
Arthur: Sure. Think of the atomic theory! Democritus introduced it, long, long ago. After that it was frequently criticized

and with excellent reasons, considering the knowledge of the time. Towards the end of the last century some continental physicists regarded it as an antediluvian monster that had no place in science. Still, it was kept alive and it was good that it was, for atomistic ideas often made excellent contributions to science. Or take the idea of the motion of the earth! It existed in antiquity; it was severely and quite reasonably criticized by Aristotle. But the memory of it survived and this was very important for Copernicus who picked it up and led it to victory. So it is good to keep refuted theories alive! It is good not to be guided by experience and experiment alone!

Jack: But what will guide us? Faith?

Arthur: No – we are scientists, so we shall try to use arguments. Now the arguments we need will take observations into account but will not give them final authority. They will assume a world that is independent of what the available observations tell us and yet supports a particular refuted view.

Jack: But this is metaphysics!

Arthur: Precisely! You have a choice – doing science in a fruitful way you can either rely on faith, or you can rely on reason. If you do the latter then you will have to become a metaphysician, metaphysics being defined as a discipline that is not based on observations but examines things independently of what observation seems to tell you. In a word – good science needs metaphysical arguments to keep it going; it would not be what it is today without this philosophical dimension . . .

Jack: Well, I'll have to think about that! At any rate – such a philosophy would be closely connected with research – but what do we have here in Plato? (points to the book) – a dialogue, a soap opera almost, lots of chatting back and forth . . .

Gaetano: Plato was a poet . . .

Jack: Well, if he was, that proves my point; this is certainly not the kind of philosophy we need!

Arnold (*to Gaetano*): I don't think you can say that Plato was a poet! He said some very harsh things about poetry. As a matter of fact, he spoke of a 'long-lasting battle between philosophy and poetry' and firmly put himself on the side of the philosophers.

Jack (*returning to the attack*): Things are worse than I thought!

He didn't like poetry and yet he didn't know how to write a decent essay, so he fell back into a boring version of poetry ...
Arnold: Stop! Stop! Let me explain! Plato is against poetry. But he is also against what you might call scientific prose and he says so quite explicitly ...
Maureen: Here in this dialogue?
Arnold: No, in another dialogue, the *Phaedrus*. A scientific essay, he implies, is largely a fraud.
Bruce: Wasn't there a paper by this title – 'Is a scientific paper a fraud?'
Arthur: Yes, you are right, by Medawar, a Nobel Prize Winner – but I don't remember where.
Arnold: At any rate – what worried Plato was that an essay gives results, perhaps some arguments, but says the same thing over and over again when you raise questions.
Arthur: Well, a written dialogue also says the same things over and over again, the only difference being that the message is told not by one character, but by many. No, the troubling thing about a scientific paper is that it tells you a fairytale. When Tom Kuhn interviewed the still living participants of the quantum revolution they at first repeated what had appeared in print. But Kuhn came well prepared. He had read letters, informal reports and all these said something very different. He mentioned the matter and slowly people remembered what had really happened. Newton, too, fits the pattern. Doing research, after all, means interacting with highly idiosyncratic material ...
Jack: There is standard experimental equipment.
Arthur: How little you logicians know about what goes on in laboratories and observatories! Standard equipment is OK for standard tinkering about: not for research that tries to push the limits a little further. Here you either use your standard equipment in a non-standard way, or you have to invent entirely new things whose side effects you are not familiar with, so you have to become acquainted with your apparatus as you do with a person and so on – nothing of which enters the traditional published accounts. But the matter is now being discussed at conferences, seminars, small meetings. Such discussions where a topic is defined and kept afloat by an ongoing debate are an absolutely necessary part of scientific know-

ledge, especially where things move very fast. A mathematician, a high energy physicist, a molecular biologist who knows only the most recent papers is not only months behind the times, he doesn't even understand what the printed work is all about; he might as well give up. I, too, have read the *Phaedrus* and it seems to me that this is precisely what Plato wanted; what he wanted was a 'live exchange', as he calls it; it is such an exchange and not some streamlined cross-section of it that defines knowledge. Naturally, he used dialogues and not scientific prose which did exist at his time and was already well developed. Still, it is not the dialogue that contains the knowledge, but the debate from which it comes and which the participant remembers when reading the dialogue. I would say that at least in this respect Plato is very modern!

Donald (*with a plaintive voice*): Can't we now start with Plato? We have a text – all this talk about science is beyond me and, besides, it doesn't belong in a seminar about epistemology. There we have to define what knowledge is ...

Maureen: I am confused, too; is this the course about ...

Leslie: ... postmodern cooking? Of course it is! But you are right. I want to hear a little more about Plato. I just looked at the last page (*he has taken a copy of the dialogue from Donald and points at a passage*) – and I find this very strange. When everything is over Socrates walks off to his trial. Wasn't he killed?

Dr Cole: Well, I think we should start at the beginning.

Seidenberg: May I say something?

Dr Cole (*looks at the ceiling in despair*).

Seidenberg: No, I think it is important. At first I thought that this gentleman here (*points to Leslie*) was not very interested in philosophy ...

Leslie: You can say that again ...

Seidenberg: No, no, but you are. Look! You turned to the last page and suddenly you became interested.

Leslie: Well, it is a little weird ...

Seidenberg: Not at all! It is true, Socrates had been accused of impiety and had to face the general assembly. Being condemned to death was one possible outcome. In another dialogue, the *Phaedo*, he has already been condemned to death, he is supposed to drink the poison at sunset, he does so and dies, right at the end of the dialogue.

Maureen (*getting less confused and quite interested*): You mean to say that Socrates talks philosophy, knowing that he is going to die?
Leslie: Weird! A professor who talks and talks although he knows that the executors are waiting for him, right outside his classroom. How does it all hang together?
Seidenberg (*excited*): Not only that. The two main characters of the dialogue Professor Cole wants to read with us, Theaetetus and Theodorus, were historical figures, both outstanding mathematicians. And Theaetetus, it says in the introduction, had been severely wounded in a battle and shortly after died from dysentery. In a way the dialogue is written in his memory. In the memory of a great mathematician who was also a valiant fighter. These are very interesting things. First, the fact that it is a dialogue; that has nothing to do with poetry in the superficial sense of pretty talk; it comes from a special conception of knowledge – and this conception is very much alive today, as Arthur said, not in (*with a glance at Jack*) 'backward subjects' but in the most respected and the most quickly developing disciplines like mathematics and high energy physics. Secondly, there is an 'existential dimension' as one might call it – the way in which the entire conversation is inserted into extreme situations of real life. I feel this is very different from large parts of modern philosophy where you analyse only the logical properties of concepts and think that is all that can be said about them.
David (*hesitatingly*): I have read the dialogue because I wanted to be prepared for this class. I, too, wondered about the ending. But I don't see that it has any effect on the debate. The debate sounds very much like a philosophy class I just had; there is somebody who says that knowledge is experience ...
Dr Cole: Perception ...
David: ... well, that knowledge is perception, somebody else has counter-examples and so on. True, the dialogue is a little long-winded – but one doesn't notice anything about death *in* it. At the end Socrates suddenly says he has to go to court. He might as well have said he is hungry and wants to have dinner. At any rate, this seems just added for effect, it doesn't give any existential dimension to the concepts ...
Seidenberg: But in the *Phaedo* ...
Charles: I have it here (*raises a book*) – I think it is even worse.

How does it start? There is Socrates with some of his admirers. And there is his wife (*reads from the book*) 'with his little boy on her arm'. She cries. 'Now,' she says, 'for the last time, your friends are going to talk to you, Socrates,' at least according to the somewhat contemptuous report given by Phaedo, the main speaker. 'She said all sorts of things women are apt to say on such occasions' – this is how he talks about her. What does Socrates do? He asks his friends to take her home so that he can talk about higher things. Quite callous I would say.
Maureen: But he is going to die!
Charles: Why should anybody be taken seriously and be permitted to act like a bastard just because he is about to die?
Bruce: And it was his own fault!
Maureen: What do you mean?
Bruce: Wasn't he supposed to address the general assembly which had condemned him but gave him a chance to defend himself? He mocked them – read the *Apology*! After that they condemned him by an even larger margin. He had as little regard for the assembly as he had for his wife and his son.
Maureen: But he died for his conviction, he did not give in.
Charles: Neither did Goering at the Nazi trial. 'Power,' he said, 'is what decides a matter – and we had a good time while it lasted.' And then he committed suicide, just like Socrates.
Seidenberg: I don't think you ought to compare people in this way.
Leslie: Why not? Both are members of the human race! Charles is quite right. Dying for your convictions does not automatically turn you into a saint. And look, what he says here – I just found the passage. What does this mean, there is a 173 on the margin . . .
Dr Cole (*wants to speak*).
Arnold (*is faster*): That is a page number of the standard edition to which scholars usually refer . . .
Leslie: Weird!
Arnold: No, quite practical. There are many editions, translations etc. etc., all different from each other. Instead of referring to an obscure translation which nobody knows but which accidentally fell into your hands you just give this one number, of the standard edition . . .
Leslie: . . . at any rate, what he seems to say here is that there is a difference between a common citizen and a philosopher.

Now I like what he says about the philosopher – 'He wanders at will from one subject to another, and from a second to a third' – that's the way we have been talking and that's why I am still here. But then he says that a 'lawyer' is always in a hurry, for there are time limits in a court. And he mocks the lawyer for being always in a hurry 'and often the race is for his life' he says. Well, I have the impression that he means not only lawyers, but common citizens as well. They don't have as much money as Plato, they have to take care of their family, their children. A way of thinking that takes a lifetime to settle simple questions is of no use for them – they would soon be starving. They have to think in a different way. Now instead of sympathizing with their predicament and appraising the solutions they found, Socrates mocks them and treats them with contempt, as he did with the assembly.
Dr Cole: Well, this is Plato, not Socrates ...
Leslie (*a little angry*): Plato, Socrates, I don't give a damn! There is an idea of philosophy, and it occurs right here in this dialogue with its 'existential dimension', and it implies that what people think and do to survive and to make their families survive deserves to be treated with contempt.
Gaetano: I think you have got something (*pulls a book from his bag*) – here, I have a German translation of the *Phaedo* with an introduction by Olof Gigon, an eminent classical scholar. He comments on Socrates sending away his wife and his little boy. What does he say? 'Both represent the world of simple, unphilosophical humanity which deserves respect but must step back when philosophy enters the stage.' 'Must step back' – that means that ordinary people lacking in philosophical refinement don't count when a philosopher, who may also be a husband, opens his mouth.
Maureen: So all this talking about death is just hot air?
Gaetano: No, I don't think so. Plato really wanted to dramatize what he thought was correct knowledge by connecting it with a new vision of death. Well, at least he has a wider horizon than (*to Jack*) your scientists ...
Charles: Every fascist has what you call a 'wider horizon' because for him science is only 'part of a larger whole', or whatever people say in this connection ...
Seidenberg (*hesitatingly*): I am a little worried by the way you have been talking about Plato. I know it is old-fashioned today

to have respect for learning and I can see the point; learning has often been misused. Still, I think you gentlemen are going a little too far. I come from a generation for whom knowledge and enlightenment were serious matters. Everybody knew that there were scholars and everybody respected them, poor people included. For us our intellectuals, our philosophers, our poets were the people who gave us light, who showed us that there were other things than the miserable lives we were leading. You see, I come from a very poor family, from the 'common people' you have been talking about; but I don't think you really know them, at least you don't know the poor people of the country I come from. 'Our son' said my parents, 'should have what we could not have, he should have an education. He should be able to read the books we only could look at from afar and we would not have understood had we held them in our hands.' And so they worked; they worked and saved their entire life so that I might have an education. I worked, too, as a bookbinder's apprentice. And there, one day, I had a fourteen-volume edition of Plato's works in my hands – a little shabby, I was supposed to prepare new covers. You cannot imagine how I felt. It was like the promised land – but so many obstacles. I certainly could not have bought and kept these books. And assume I had bought them, would I have understood? I opened one of the volumes and found a passage where Socrates was speaking. I do not remember what he said, but I do remember that I felt as if he were talking to me, in a kind, gentle and somewhat mocking way. And then came the Nazis. There were already some students who favoured Nazism and, I am sorry to say gentlemen, they talked very much like you – with contempt in their voice. These are new times, they said, so let's forget about all these ancient writers! I agree that Plato often avoids trivial matters and occasionally mocks them. But I don't think he mocks the people who are part of it; he mocks the sophists who dogmatically say that this is all there is. For the common people themselves, at least the common people I know, are not like this. They hope for a better life, if not for themselves then at least for their children. You know, there is an interesting thing about dates of the dialogues. The first dialogues Plato wrote after the death of Socrates had nothing to do with his demise. They were comedies like the *Euthydemus* or the *Ion*, full of wit and mockery. The *Apology*, the *Phaedo* and the *Theaetetus* came later, presumably after Plato had digested the Pythagorean doctrine of an after-life. And so death now assumes a different aspect – it is a beginning, not an end. And it is true that Socrates, the real Socrates, did not swallow democracy line, hook and sinker, as you say in your language. He saw that there were problems. It is reported that he mocked democracy as an institution where a donkey becomes a horse when sufficiently many people vote accordingly. Well, is this not a problem we face today? When we discuss the role of science in society and, especially, in a democracy? Not everything can be decided by vote – but where is the boundary and who is going to draw it? For Plato the answer was clear: the people who have studied the matter, the wise men, they are going to draw the boundary! My parents and I thought exactly the same. Of course, Plato had money and more time – but don't hold this against him! He did not spend his money like other people in his class, on intrigues, horse-racing and political powerplay. He loved Socrates who was poor, ugly and uncouth. He wrote about him, not only to honour him, but to lay the foundations for a better life much in the way in which the modern peace movement is striving for a better life. Remember – this was the time of the Peloponnesian war, of political murder; democracy was overthrown, reinstated, intrigued against. So, what I wanted to say is that we should be grateful to these people instead of mocking them . . .

Lee Feng: I understand what you want to say, sir, and I am in complete sympathy, not only because I think that a community or a nation needs wise men but also because I think that a life without a trace of reverence for anything is a rather shallow life. But I see a problem when this reverence is not balanced by a little healthy scepticism. I think the recent history of my country is a good example . . .

Gaetano: But there are examples much closer to home; they may be rather trivial compared with what you (*to Lee Feng*) are talking about, but I think they are the reason why Leslie and Charles have reacted so violently. Some of the professors here and some of the graduate students talk about the leading lights in their profession as if they were gods; they cannot write a line without quoting Nietzsche, or Heidegger, or Derrida, and their whole life seems to consist in bouncing back and forth between a few icons. You sir (*to Seidenberg*) most likely lived at a time and in a community where people had a personal relation to their wise men and to what they said. I don't think there exists such a personal relation today, there is much pressure to conform and, above all, instead of the living discourse Plato wants we have empty phrases arranged in a schematic way. This is a hateful phenomenon – small wonder that Leslie and Charles explode when they see something similar, or apparently similar in an ancient author. And then there is something else – the democratic way of looking at people – the way in which the Athenians seem to have looked at Socrates. 'Yes, this Socrates,' they seem to have said, – 'we know him; he is a little silly, he has nothing better to do than standing around and bothering people – but he is not really a bad guy and occasionally he says some very clever things.' They laughed about him when they saw him on the stage, in Aristophanes' *Clouds* – and Socrates seems to have laughed with them. Respect is mixed with scepticism and, occasionally, ridicule. We can go even further. If we can trust Heraclitus, then the people of Ephesus said something like this: we don't want anybody who is the best in our midst – let such a person live elsewhere and with other people. I think such an attitude makes excellent sense. It does not mean that all people with special knowledge will be thrown out – only those who because of their special knowledge want special treatment! At any rate, mockery is a thousand times better than either murder or a deadly serious criticism that elevates the critic by the stature it gives to the person criticized – obviously you cannot become great by attacking idiots. I suspect that this is the real reason why writers without talent dwell on other writers without talent and insist that they be taken seriously.

Dr Cole: I think we have moved rather far away from our topic. Besides, you can't judge an author from a few lines torn out of context. So, why don't we start reading the dialogue in a more coherent way and decide about its merits afterwards? Plato has some very interesting things to say about knowledge – for example, about relativism. No doubt you have heard about relativism.

Charles: You mean Feyerabend?

Dr Cole (*shocked*): No, certainly not. But there are competent people who think they have arguments to show that whatever you say and whatever reasons you give for what you say depends on a 'cultural context', that is, on the way of life in which you participate.
Lee Feng: Does this mean that scientific laws are not universally true?
Dr Cole: Yes! They are correct if you belong to the Western civilization, they are correct relative to the procedures and standards developed by this civilization – but they are not only not true but make no sense in a different culture.
Jack: Because people don't understand them.
Dr Cole: No, not just because they don't understand them but because their criteria for evaluating what makes sense and what does not make sense are different. Being presented with Kepler's laws they not only say 'What does it mean?' – they say 'This is gibberish'.
Bruce: Has anybody asked them?
Dr Cole: I do not know – but this is irrelevant; the relativists are here making a logical point.
Jack: You mean they don't say 'The Afar, when presented with Newton's theory, say "This is nonsense"', but 'Judged by the criteria implicit in the system of thought developed by the Afar, Newton's theory is nonsense'.
Dr Cole: Yes.
Jack: Which assumes that the Afar or, for that matter, any culture has a 'system of thought' that can be used to make such judgements.
Dr Cole: Of course.
Jack: But do they? And isn't that an empirical question? And who has investigated this empirical question?
Dr Cole: Linguists and sociologists.
Jack: Now, if Newton's theory is nonsense for a culture, or a period, then how can people of this culture ever learn it and how did the theory itself ever come into existence?
Bruce: There are revolutions – haven't you read Kuhn's book? Transitions between different ways of thinking revolutionize standards, basic principles, the lot.
Jack: Now that's just a word! I don't know Kuhn very well but I wonder how such a revolution proceeds. Don't people argue during a revolution?

Bruce: They do.
Jack: Do they make sense?
Dr Cole: In a way, no.
Charles (*contemptuously*): And by 'in a way' you mean: according to the view that arguments make sense only relative to a system.
Dr Cole: Yes.
Charles: But Jack has questioned this view, so you can't use it to answer what Jack has asked, namely: do transitional arguments make sense? You have to find an answer in a different way.
Dr Cole: How?
Charles: For example, by examining how people reacted to such arguments.
Dr Cole: Well, one thing history teaches us is that new groups form, old groups die out . . .
Charles: Do you mean to say this proves that transitional arguments have no force?
Dr Cole: It is not a matter of argument any more, but a matter of conversion. New groups form and they have new standards.
Charles: Not so fast! First of all, your facts are not right. For example, many people who had been Aristotelians became Copernicans when they either read Copernicus or Galileo, or heard Galileo talk. There were of course new groups, but these groups had argued their way out of their old beliefs by means of procedures they still retained. There was not a complete change of 'system'. Secondly, assume it is a matter of conversion – what are these people being converted to? Either the system is already there, then we have no conversion, or it is not there, then the conversion is to nothing. No, things cannot be that simple. What I would say is that transitional arguments do make sense, not to all people, for there is no argument that makes sense to everybody; they make sense to some and this means that the view that there are 'systems' and that they alone give meaning to what is being said must be wrong.
Jack: That is exactly what I wanted to say. The cogency of an argument depends on standards and a revolution changes these. So it seems either that a revolution cannot be based on arguments, or the cogency of arguments does not depend on a 'system of thought' – and if the latter, then relativism is false. On the other hand, if it is true then we are forever stuck in a

system until a miracle gives us another system, and then we are stuck in that one. A strange view!
Donald: Does Plato discuss this view?
Dr Cole: He discusses one of the first relativists in Western history, Protagoras.
Bruce: Well, hasn't relativism advanced a little since then?
Dr Cole: Yes and no. The basic position is still very similar to that of Protagoras, but there are now lots of protective devices which make the matter seem more difficult than it really is.
Bruce: You mean – Protagoras says the same as modern relativists, but he says it in a simpler way.
Dr Cole: You might say that. But let's now finally start with the dialogue!
Lee Feng: Where, please?
Dr Cole: Here, at 146 ... Socrates asks Theaetetus to define knowledge.
Arthur: I find this absurd.
Jack: What do you mean?
Arthur: Trying to define knowledge.
Jack: That is standard procedure, in the sciences and elsewhere. You have a long expression that's inconvenient, so you decide to introduce an abbreviation and the sentence that says what abbreviates what is the definition.
Arthur: But the situation here is the inverse of what you have been describing! Knowledge already exists, there are the arts and crafts, the various professions, Theodorus and Theaetetus have a sizeable amount of mathematical knowledge and now Theaetetus is supposed to characterize this big unwieldy assembly by a short formula. It's not a matter of abbreviating a long formula, but of finding a common property for the elements of a chequered assembly which, moreover, are constantly changing.
Jack: Well, we have to draw a line somewhere, especially today and with people around who want to revive astrology, witchcraft, magic. Some things are knowledge, others are not – do you agree to that?
Arthur: Sure. But I don't believe you can draw the line once and for all, and with the help of a simple formula. I don't even think you can draw it, like a traffic law. Boundaries emerge, fade, disappear again as part of a very complex historical process ...

Jack: But this is not so. Philosophers often drew lines, and defined knowledge ...
Arthur: ... and who used their definitions? Look. Newton drew a line when he defended his research in optics and immediately crossed it. Research is much too complicated to follow simple lines. And Theaetetus knows this! Socrates asks: 'What is knowledge?' Theaetetus replies ...
Donald: Where?
Arthur: Somewhere in the middle of 146. Well, he replies that knowledge is 'all the sciences which I learn from Theodorus – geometry and those which you just mentioned' – he is talking of astronomy and harmony and arithmetic. And, he continues, 'I would include the art of the cobbler and other craftsmen; these, each and all of them are knowledge.' This is a perfectly good reply: knowledge is a complex matter, it is different in different areas and so the best answer to 'What is knowledge?' is a list. I myself would add details and mention the various schools that exist within each subject. At any rate, the idea that knowledge and, for that matter, science can be captured in a simple formula is a chimaera.
Arnold: It is not a chimaera, it has been done. For example one characterization is that knowledge is what can be criticized.
Bruce: But everything can be criticized, not only knowledge.
Arnold: Well, I have to be more specific: a claim to knowledge exists only if the person making the claim can say in advance under what circumstances he would withdraw the claim.
Leslie: That's not a definition of 'knowledge' but of 'claim to knowledge'.
Arthur: I don't mind, on the contrary, I can now state my objection even more clearly: according to your definition of 'claim to knowledge' most scientific theories are not such claims for, given a complicated theory, scientists hardly ever know in advance what particular circumstances will make them give it up. Theories very often contain hidden assumptions one is not even aware of. New developments bring these assumptions to the fore – and then the criticism can begin.
Lee Feng: Do you have an example?
Bruce: Yes – the assumption of infinite signal velocities became known only with the special theory of relativity. In your definition you are supposed to say in 1690 what will happen to Newton's theory in 1919 – and that's absurd. It is the same

kind of absurdity that is contained in the demand for a definition of 'knowledge'. New subjects are constantly entering the scene, old subjects change, which means that the definition will be both very long, with lots of qualifications, and that it will be subjected to change.
Arnold: But you have to have a criterion to separate fake subjects from genuine subjects and you have to formulate this criterion independently of what subjects exist – how else can you judge them in an objective way?
Arthur: 'In an objective way' – these are mere words. Don't you think that something as decisive as the criteria that define knowledge must be examined very carefully? And if they are being examined, then we have research about criteria and this research will itself be guided by criteria – you simply cannot put yourself outside knowledge and research. Besides, assume you have a criterion. That is not enough. You also want to have something that agrees with the criterion – otherwise your criterion is empty. Hardly anybody today will spend much time on finding the correct definition of 'unicorn'.
Arnold: I am quite prepared to admit that my criterion may expose everything as a fraud . . .
Bruce: Well, won't you go on using some of these fraudulent things and separate them from other fraudulent things? For example, won't you continue trusting some physicians more than others? Or trusting an astronomer who has predicted a solar eclipse but not an astrologist who predicted an earthquake? If you do, then your criterion is itself exposed as a fraud; if not, you will soon be dead.
David: But some definitions are needed for legal purposes. For example, the laws that separate church and state and demand that science but not religious views be taught in public schools. Wasn't there a case where fundamentalists tried to introduce some of their ideas into elementary school education calling them scientific theories?
Arthur: Yes, in Arkansas. Experts testified, gave some simple definitions, and that settled the matter.
Charles: Well, that only shows that legal practice is in need of improvement.
Donald: Can't we get back to the dialogue? You say a list is OK. But Socrates objects!
Arthur: What is his objection?

Maureen: He wants one thing, not many.
Bruce: That's what we have just been talking about – he can't have his definition *and* something of substance.
Maureen: But there is this one word, 'knowledge'; so why not one thing?
Arnold: 'Circle' is one word, but there is the geometrical circle; the circle of friends who don't have to sit around in a geometrical circle; circular reasoning i.e. reasoning that assumes what is to be proved but without moving on a geometrical circle . . .
Maureen: Well, that is not the same! There is one genuine circle and the other things are, well, what do you call them . . .
Gaetano: Metaphors?
Lee Feng: Analogies?
Leslie It does not matter – one word, many meanings, many things. And Socrates assumes such things never happen . . .
Gaetano: Besides, in the passage before the question . . .
Leslie: Where?
Gaetano: Towards the end of 145 – but you won't find it in the English, you have to consult the Greek – he already uses three different words, *episteme* (and the corresponding verb), *sophia* (and two further forms of the same root) and *manthanein*.
Leslie (*gently mocking Seidenberg*): Your great and wise Plato!
Lee Feng: But Theaetetus himself suggests how knowledge might be unified. True, what Socrates says is not only dogmatic but also incoherent. Now Theaetetus tries to make sense of it and in a rather interesting way. To prepare his suggestion he describes a mathematical discovery he and his friend made some time ago.
Donald: I tried to understand that passage, but I have no idea what it is all about.
Lee Feng: But it is very simple, really. Here, let's start in the middle of 147, 147d3, to be precise.
Leslie: What does that mean?
Arnold: It means page 147 of the standard edition – remember? – section d of the page (every page of the standard edition is subdivided into sections for convenience), line 3.
Lee Feng (*reads*): 'Theodorus was drawing diagrams to show us something about squares . . .'
Donald: It doesn't say that in my text . . .

Leslie: Not in mine either. Here it says: 'Theodorus was writing out for us something about roots ...'
Dr Cole: Well, we were going to run into this problem sooner or later – not all translations say the same thing.
Donald: Don't the translators know Greek?
Dr Cole: They do and they don't. The Greek of Plato is not a living language, so we have to rely on texts. Now different authors often use the same words in different ways, that's why we have not only lexica about ancient Greek, but special lexica for Homer, Herodotus, Plato, Aristotle and others. Moreover, we are here dealing with a mathematical passage and the person speaking is a mathematician. Mathematicians often use ordinary terms in a technical sense and it is not always clear what the sense is. *Dynamis*, the word which is translated as 'root' in your text, usually means power, force; it also occurs in economics. It took scholars a long time to figure out that here it most likely means a square. Problems like this one will arise with all the more difficult passages.
Donald: What can we do?
Dr Cole: Learn Greek.
Donald: Learn Greek?
Dr Cole: Well, or be prepared to discover that what you are getting is just a very bowdlerized account of what is 'really' going on. (*To Lee Feng*) Your translation seems to be by somebody who knew of the special difficulties of our passage ...
Lee Feng (*looking at his text*): It's by a certain McDowell.
Dr Cole: Ah, John – well, he certainly knows what he is doing, at least at this place. Continue!
Lee Feng: 'Theodorus was drawing diagrams to show us something about squares – namely that a square of three square feet and one of five square feet aren't commensurable, in respect of length of side, with a square of one square foot ...'
Donald: What does it mean, commensurable?
Lee Feng: Assume you have a square of three square feet. Then the side of this square cannot be expressed by a finite decimal fraction, or, more simply, by a fraction with an integer in the numerator and another, however large, in the denominator.
Donald: How do you know that?
Dr Cole: There is a proof for this ...
Arthur: As a matter of fact, there are various kinds of proof ...
Dr Cole: ... and some of them were known already in antiquity.

Quite simple proofs, but I don't think we should go into that. Just accept that there are such proofs, that they were known to Theodorus and that he illustrated them by diagrams.
Lee Feng (*continues*): '... with a square of one square foot; and so on, selecting each case individually, up to seventeen square feet.'
Jack: Does this mean he had a different proof for each of these numbers?
Dr Cole: Yes. Like Theaetetus in the case of knowledge he gave a list of irrational numbers, starting with the square root of three, each number associated with a different proof.
Jack: So, if there had been one single proof, the same for any number which, applied to the number, showed it to be irrational or not, then this proof would have been a general criterion of irrationality.
Lee Feng: That is the point. But Theaetetus does something different. He divides all numbers into two classes, one containing numbers of the form A times A, the other numbers of the form A times B, with A different from B, A and B being integers and he calls the numbers of the first kind square numbers and the numbers of the second kind oblong numbers.
Jack: Aha, and the sides of squares whose area is given by a square number ...
Lee Feng: These he calls 'lengths' ...
Jack: ... are rational numbers, the sides of squares whose area is given by an oblong number ...
Lee Feng: ... which he calls powers ...
Jack: ... are irrational numbers. So, in this terminology, irrational numbers are classified as powers, no longer enumerated one by one. Quite ingenious.
Leslie: And Socrates wants the same for knowledge?
Dr Cole: Yes, he does.
Bruce: But knowledge is not like numbers.
Dr Cole: That's exactly what Theaetetus says.
Bruce: And he is right. Numbers are pretty simple, transparent and they don't change. Knowledge can be rather complicated, it always changes and different people say different things about it. In a way the difference between numbers and knowledge is like the difference between basic physics, where you have simple and general laws, and meteorology, for example, where you try now one trick, now another. Besides, know-

ledge isn't just there, it is made by people, it is like a work of art ...
David: You mean knowledge is a social science ...
Bruce: Not a social science, but a social phenomenon. Now it seems that Socrates wants all domains of knowledge to be like mathematics where you have general concepts covering many different cases and theorems about these cases. Well, how does Socrates reply to Theaetetus?
David (*looking at the text*): He talks a lot about being a midwife – wait a minute – now he's got Theaetetus where he wants him, he finally gives a definition: knowledge is perception!
Maureen: And there is no debate?
David (*looking again*): No, Socrates just insists on a definition and Theaetetus finally gives him one.
Arnold: Don't be too hard on Theaetetus, he was only 16 years old when the dialogue was supposed to have taken place.
Bruce: No, I am talking about Socrates. The problem is not discussed, it is taken for granted that knowledge, all of it, not only the mathematical parts, is like mathematics ...
Dr Cole: Not quite. If we ever come to the end of the dialogue you will see that we are left without a definition. Three definitions are proposed, three definitions are refuted and then Socrates has to go to court. Some later philosophers counted Plato among the sceptics, just for this reason. Carneades, one of the later leaders of the school, was even a sceptic himself.
Leslie: But isn't the *Theaetetus* later than the *Republic*?
Dr Cole: It is. You are right. That is the general assumption. In the *Republic* the matter of knowledge seems to be settled, more or less. In the *Theaetetus* it is again up in the air and much later, in the *Timaeus* the theory of the *Republic* is called a blueprint which has to be checked against the actual and imperfect shape and development of humans, societies and the entire universe. So what we have to look at is not just one dialogue, but the entire sequence.
Maureen: Isn't anything settled in this dialogue we are reading?
Dr Cole: Some things are, for example the matter of relativism.
Charles: You mean Protagoras?
Dr Cole: Yes.

Charles: But that starts very badly. Theaetetus says 'Knowledge is perception', Socrates replies 'That's the opinion of Protagoras' and then he quotes him: 'Man is the measure of all things, of those that are that they are and of those that are not that they are not ...'
Donald: Why don't you stick to the text? It says here 'of the existence of things that are'.
Dr Cole: Remember, that is a translation! And in this case the translator has given us a paraphrase ...
Donald: A paraphrase?
Dr Cole: Well, he has not translated word for word which would sound a little awkward in English, but has used a more elegant way of expressing matters. Many translators do that; Plato occasionally uses long descriptions for things for which some translators think they have a simple term. But often Plato himself did not have the term, so their translation is anachronistic on top of being just a paraphrase. For all these reasons we should be very careful with phrases like 'Plato says this' or 'Plato says that' ...
Charles: But Plato himself is not very careful. Protagoras speaks of 'man' – I guess he means any human being.
Dr Cole: Yes, in Greek and in Latin you have different words for a human being – *anthropos* in Greek, *homo* in Latin and for a man – *aner* in Greek, *vir* in Latin.
Charles: And he says that a human being is a measure of all things – he does not say how the human being measures – it can be perception, it can be intuition, it can be past experience.
Arnold: But we have some other indications. Aristotle, for example, says that according to Protagoras the tangent does not cut a circle in one point, but in more than one; that sounds like he is relying on perception.
Charles: Well, any quantum theoretician would say the same but not because his perception tells him so and, besides, look at 167, where Socrates lets Protagoras explain his views more fully. Here the Socratean Protagoras compares the teacher with a physician. A physician heals the sick, he says, by using medicine. The sick person perceives that he is in a bad shape and correctly says, according to Protagoras, that he is in a bad shape. The physician changes the bad condition of the patient

to a better condition – he does not change true to false, for the patient's judgement, being the measure of things, is always true. In the same way, says Protagoras, good rhetoricians 'make the good instead of the evil seem just to a city' or, as I would rather say, to the inhabitants of a city. Now Good and Evil, Just and Injust are not perceptual terms – people judge Good and Evil in a very different way, but they judge it, and are therefore measures of it. So Plato himself gives an account of Protagoras that contradicts the identification of this measure principle with the idea that knowledge is perception. Turning Protagoras into a naive empiricist is simply slander.
Leslie: But here is the example of the wind which seems cold to one, warm to another ...
Maureen: Well, this may be just an example.
Leslie: And the idea that everything always changes ...
Charles: That, too, does not follow from what Protagoras says about man being a measure. On the contrary, 'measuring' their surroundings, some people find that things always remain the same and get bored ...
Maureen: And there are the sciences, a human product, discovering regularities and repetitions.
Arnold: And there is another dialogue, the *Protagoras*, where Protagoras appears in person and recommends that people who violate the laws of a city eventually be put to death. The city has 'measured' that too much change is bad, it has decided to introduce laws to guarantee some kind of stability and it defends these laws, if necessary by executing repeated offenders.
Leslie: And this guy is called a relativist?
Dr Cole: Well, you see, you must be very careful with general terms like 'relativist', 'rationalist', 'empiricist' – and so on.
Donald: But it does make sense to connect Protagoras with change. Man is a measure, but man constantly changes ...
Charles: Not according to me who measures what is going on in me and around me! Of course I change here and there, but I keep many views, I improve them, find better arguments for them, for the same views ...
Arnold: And who is going to decide that?
Charles: I, of course, according to Protagoras.
Jack: I think the matter is not quite so simple. What you are

saying is that Plato quite arbitrarily connects Protagoras with the doctrine of change. But look here at this example at 154 ...

Donald: The dice?

Jack: Yes.

Donald: Now that I did not understand at all!

Jack: You will, if you approach it with certain assumptions in your mind. There are six dice – they are more than four dice and less than twelve dice. Now we did not take anything away from the six, the six remained the same and yet they became less.

Donald: That's trivial – 'greater' and 'less' are relations.

Jack: Aha! So what we have are stable things, six dice here, four dice and twelve dice there, and different relations between them. Now the measure doctrine of Protagoras also introduces a relation, between what is and the activity of measuring. But here we have no stable entities with relations between them, the situation is the other way around – everything THAT IS is being constituted by the relation: the measuring makes it BE. And so I think that what Socrates now says at 153d3ff is entirely appropriate. In the case of seeing you neither can say that the colour you see IS in your eyes or IS outside of it, or anywhere, for that matter; you must say that it and its place both come into existence during the process of perception – they are part of an indivisible block uniting what is with what is being perceived.

Lee Feng: Einstein-Podolsky-Rosen correlations!

Donald: What?

Lee Feng: This is exactly what the quantum theory says about the process of measurement. There was a thought experiment which Einstein and his collaborators introduced to prove, just like Plato wants to prove, that things have definite properties even before they are being measured. They imagine a very special situation in which there are two particles and we know the sum of their momenta and the difference of their positions ...

Donald: I don't understand a word – and what has this got to do with Plato?

Charles: Well, it depends on how you want to discuss a philosopher. Do you just want to see how well he deals with his

opponent, given the knowledge of his time, or do you want to know to what extent his ideas returned at a later age? The first approach is very interesting but I think the second is even more so. After all, an argument is like a battle. One party is defeated – given the weapons of the time. But the weapons constantly change. We learn new things, our mathematics becomes more complicated in one respect, much simpler in another – what took pages and pages of proof before can now be dealt with in a line or two – our experimental equipment changes, and so on. So an idea defeated today may be an idea proved to be right tomorrow – think of the idea that the earth moves. Now it is very interesting that Plato in his attempt to refute Protagoras produces a theory of perception which shows, at least to us, to what extent Protagoras anticipated a twentieth-century theory.
Donald: But what is this twentieth-century theory?
Lee Feng: Well, that is a little difficult – but let me try. No doubt you have heard of the uncertainty relations.
Leslie: Yes, Hasenberg.
Lee Feng: Heisenberg. Well, expressed simply the relations say that you can't know both the position and the momentum ...
Donald: What is 'momentum'?
Lee Feng: Something like velocity – simply think of it as a velocity. At any rate – you can't know both the position and the momentum of a particle with absolute precision. If you know the one very well, the other becomes more vague and vice versa. Now you can interpret these relations in various ways. For example, you can say: the particle always is at a precise place and has a precise velocity but you cannot know both of them because any measurement you perform of the one changes what you might know about the other.
Arnold: So, if I know the position of a particle very well and try to measure its velocity, this attempt will annihilate my knowledge of the position?
Lee Feng: You might say that.
Leslie: Weird!
Lee Feng: Now there is another interpretation of the uncertainty relations. It says that it is the particle itself, not our knowledge of it that becomes indefinite. For example, if by some trick you can determine its momentum with absolute

precision, then you not only don't know anything about its position, there doesn't even exist anything like a position any more.
Donald: So, it's not a particle.
Lee Feng: You might say that. And what I just said of position and momentum applies to many other pairs of physical magnitudes, for example to the x- and the y-component of the spin of a particle. A pair of magnitudes that cannot be precise together is called a pair of complementary magnitudes. Position and momentum are complementary in this sense or, rather, any component of position in a certain direction is complementary to the component of momentum in the same direction. Now Einstein and his collaborators constructed a case ...
Charles: A thought experiment?
Lee Feng: Yes, it was a thought experiment when Einstein first introduced it – it has since become a real experiment. Well, Einstein constructed a special case by which he tried to show that the quantum theory itself, taken together with some trivial assumptions, implies that complementary magnitudes do have simultaneous sharp values. I shall try to explain the argument – but you must stop me if you don't understand.
Leslie: Don't worry, we sure will.
Lee Feng: Einstein assumes two particles, R and S, and he assumes that we know their distance as well as the sum of their momenta.
Donald: But we can't know the location and the speed at the same time – you just said that!
Lee Feng: You are completely right. However, we can know certain combinations of the two, for example the *difference* of the locations for two particles which is their distance, and the *sum* of their momenta – these two we can know with absolute precision.
David: How come?
Lee Feng: Well, just take it from me that we can – otherwise we never get off the ground. Now assume that R stays with us and that S moves so far away that it is no longer affected by anything we do in the surroundings of R. Now we measure the position of R – which we can do with absolute precision.
Bruce: No measurement has absolute precision – there is always some error.

Lee Feng: Remember, this is a thought experiment dealing with the quantum theory! 'Absolute precision' now means that no quantum theoretical law is contradicted when such precision is attained. So, we measure the position of R – we know the distance of R and S and we can infer not only the position of S *after* the measurement but also its position *immediately before* the measurement because S is so far away that carrying out a measurement on R cannot have influenced it in any way. And we can also say, for the same reason, that S *always had a well-defined position*, whether we measured it or not, because the measurement could have been carried out at any time. The same argument applied to velocity tells us that S *always had a well-defined momentum* – so it always had a well defined position and a well-defined momentum, contrary to the second interpretation of the uncertainty relations I gave above.
Jack: Well, we obviously have to drop that interpretation.
Lee Feng: But we cannot! It was introduced for a reason. It is the only interpretation capable of reconciling apparently conflicting experimental results.
Leslie: Well, then we simply have to say that a measurement affects an object even if it is very far away . . .
Charles: Which is very similar to the example of the dice – things change although nothing is added and nothing taken away . . .
Lee Feng: Unless you do the same thing we did there – declare position and momentum to be relations, not properties inherent in particles, and not simply relations between things that have stable properties apart from the relations but relations between things part of whose properties are being constituted by an interaction – exactly as in the theory of vision Plato develops and attributes to Protagoras. I think this is very interesting for it shows that Plato's arguments against Protagoras may also be turned against quantum mechanics which, however, is pretty well established.
Donald: Well, I certainly have no idea of what you are talking about! But I did read the dialogue and Socrates has some very neat refutations of this idea which you connect with quantum mechanics. Take only one: the thesis is 'Knowledge is perception'. Now, I look at you, I perceive you, and I know that you are there. I close my eyes, I still know that you are there though I don't perceive you any longer. 'Thus, then,' Socrates

concludes, 'the assertion that knowledge and perception are one involves a manifest impossibility.' Now what do you say to that?
David (excited): That you haven't read far enough. Just go down a few more lines!
Donald: Where?
David: After the line you just quoted! What does it say?
Donald (reads): 'Like a good-for-nothing cock, without having won the victory, we walk away from the argument and crow.' I don't understand this.
Bruce: It is very simple. He says that the arguments he produced so far are a sham.
Donald: Why would he do such a thing – first construct lots of counter-arguments, for this is not the only one, and then say they are worthless?
Dr Cole: Because that was what the sophists were doing and he wanted to expose their manner of arguing.
Donald: You mean, using counter-examples?
Dr Cole: Exactly.
Donald: But isn't that what one does in the sciences, suggesting hypotheses and using counter-examples to falsify them?
Jack: It all depends! Take 'All ravens are black'. How is that refuted?
Donald: By a white raven.
Jack: I dream about a white raven.
Donald: No, a real white raven.
Jack: I paint a raven white.
Donald: Not a painted raven, obviously!
Jack: Now that's exactly what Socrates says. Closing our eyes we still *know* but do *not perceive* and so knowledge cannot be perception – this was the argument. Looking at a painted raven we see that it is a *raven* but it is *not black* and so not all ravens are black. What is the mistake? We were guided by the agreement or disagreement of *words*. In the case of the ravens it is not enough to find that there is a raven correctly described by the *word* 'white', we also have to know what kind of whiteness we want – and that is not a simple matter (assume a bunch of ravens lost colour because of some sickness – how shall we deal with this event?). In the case of knowledge it does not suffice to find that there is non-perceptual knowledge, we have to decide what kind of non-perception we want. Now

a philosopher who identifies knowledge with perception (and there are some doubts Protagoras did this) may have a very sophisticated notion of perception, and so we have to go a little further into his theory. For example, he most likely will not assume that memory (in a simple sense) and perception are about the same thing for he will have a theory of memory as complicated as the theory of perception Lee Feng here just connected with the quantum theory.

Donald: Does this mean that falsification does not work?

Charles: Oh no, it does work, but it is a rather complex process. Simple counter-examples do not suffice – they may be as chimaerical as the painted raven and note, this is a conceptual matter! What we are talking about are not observations but the kinds of entities connected with them; we are talking metaphysics! Any good refutation involves metaphysical judgements! What Socrates says is that a new theory will arrange things in a new way, hence refuting it by a comparison with words adapted to the old arrangement is an unfair kind of criticism. The criticism of Einstein, Podolsky and Rosen was an unfair criticism in precisely this sense.

Donald (depressed): So we have to start all over again.

Dr Cole: Yes, we do (*looking at his watch*) – but I think we should now proceed a little more quickly, there is not much time left and next time I want to go on and discuss John Searle. So, let me just enumerate the second set of criticisms Socrates produces . . .

Donald: And these are now real criticisms, not sham criticisms?

Dr Cole: Yes, they are. The first criticism is about the future.

Maureen: But that comes much later.

Dr Cole: Well, I prefer to deal with it now, because it is a very simple matter. Turn to 177, the end, over to 178. According to Protagoras good laws are those most citizens think are good laws. But the citizens also think that good laws are laws that make the city flourish – that is why they are introduced. Now what happens when laws that seemed to be good to the lawgivers and therefore were good for them turn out to be the ruin of the city?

Leslie: What happens when objectively good laws turn out to be the ruin of the city?

Donald: What do you mean?

Leslie: Well, Plato obviously had some alternative in mind. He attacks Protagoras because he believes that Platonic ideas are better than Protagorean opinions. But Platonic ideas face exactly the same problem. There they are, true, objectively valid, to use this word which always turns up when some people want to suppress others but don't want to take personal responsibility for it – and the result is disaster.

Dr Cole: Well, let us assume you are right. Plato himself has a problem. But isn't there also a problem for Protagoras?

Jack: I don't think so. Some years ago people said 'These laws seem good to us, and therefore they are good for us'. Now they say 'These laws seem bad to us, and therefore they are bad for us'. There is no contradiction, just as there is no contradiction between my saying 'I am feeling good and therefore I am in a good condition' on Tuesday and 'I am feeling bad and therefore I am in a bad condition' on Wednesday.

Arnold: But if that is so, then I see quite a different problem. How can people ever have a debate? To have a debate A must be able to say something that contradicts what B says, which means that what A and B say must be independent of their state of mind.

Jack: No. To have a debate it suffices that it seems to A that what B says differs from what he says. Besides, this condition is also necessary: if A and B contradict each other 'objectively' but neither notices it, then we don't have a debate. Platonic ideas must leave a trace in the world in which we live but once they do we can go on without them.

Maureen: But how can you persuade a person, when this is how you think, and why will you want to persuade anybody?

Jack: I think Protagoras gives an answer to this when he compares the rhetorician with a physician, but with a physician who uses words, not pills, as his medicine. A philosopher finds a person he thinks is in need of improvement. He approaches the person and talks to him. If he does his job well, then the talk will work like a medicine and will change both the ideas and the general attitude of the person who seemed so misguided.

Maureen: But this last statement, namely 'The talk will work like a medicine', is something that just is, but does not appear to anybody.

Jack: Oh no! If the philosopher does his job well, then it will

appear both to him and to his patient that the medicine has worked, and it will also appear so to a sociologist who investigates the matter – though nobody needs him as the philosopher and his pupil can reach agreement without such additional information.
Maureen: You mean, the final criterion is that both are feeling good?
Bruce: Well, isn't that true of all theoretical debates? You have some highly abstract theory, say Hegel in philosophy, or supergravity in physics. People talk to each other. You watch the conversation from the distance. You don't understand a word but you see that things proceed smoothly – people disagree, but they seem to know what they are doing. It seems to you they know what they are talking about though for you it is utter gibberish. Now, objective or no, the criterion of understanding you use in practical life and also in highly abstract subjects is that the whole matter opens up to you and that you are able to swim in it without resistance.
Jack: You can say the same things about physical theory. There is theory, there are experiments ...
Lee Feng: All these things can be done by computers ...
Jack: Yes, they can, but the question is – why have all this equipment? – and here personal judgements come in ...
Lee Feng: Yes, at the periphery ...
Jack: It does not matter *where* they occur – they are decisive! If scientists suddenly get bored with what they are doing, or if they start hallucinating, everyone in his own way, or if the general public turns to mysticism, then science will collapse like a house of cards. Now the personal judgements that maintain physics are often so hidden and so automatic that all seems to be calculation and experiment. As a matter of fact I would say that it is this very thoughtlessness that creates the impression of objectivity! Either way personal judgement or lack of judgement is involved. I think there even exists a book by a physicist ...
Arthur: A physical chemist – Michael Polanyi; are you speaking of his book *Personal Knowledge* ...
Maureen: I have been very worried by this conversation. Everything seems to come down to the impressions people have. But then I am not dealing with anybody apart from myself ...

Arnold: You mean solipsism, the idea that you alone exist and everything else is just a colourful part of your personality?
Maureen: Yes, but that cannot possibly be the whole truth.
Leslie: Are you sure?
Jack: At any rate – Protagoras would not say it is! He would say, stretching out his hand, that there was his hand, that his hand was different from his thought of the hand and that both were different from the person standing in front of him. But he would add that he knew all this from his own personal experience and that he had no other source for it. Why, even if he says 'I read it in a book' – he still has to rely on his impression of the book – and so on.
Maureen: But does this not mean he knows only the surface of people – only what strikes him about them . . .
Gaetano: Well, let me turn the thing around! Do you ever know more than the surface of people? Let me ask you. Did it ever happen to you that you saw a friend of yours, either from nearby, or from the distance, without realizing that it was your friend?
Maureen: Yes, that did happen to me and it was rather disconcerting. I once saw a very good friend of mine standing at a distance in a library and I thought 'What an unpleasant looking person!' – then I recognized him.
Gaetano: And what happened?
Maureen: Well, he is a very sweet person – and that's how he looked when I recognized him.
Gaetano: And what about the other impression?
Maureen: That was just an accident.
Gaetano: You mean, because it lasted such a short time?
Maureen: Yes.
Gaetano: And you are sure that other people won't ever see him that way?
Maureen: Well, I don't really know; it was a very upsetting experience!
Gaetano: But this experience, and your other experience, and your memories – isn't that all you have?
Maureen: Yes.
Gaetano: And obtaining knowledge means creating some kind of order in this assembly . . .
Dr Cole: I think it will be better if we return to the dialogue, for some of your questions may find an answer in there. I think

Plato would say that people are not always able to create the right kind of order – that it needs an expert to do that. That is his main point. Not everybody judges – experts do. For example (*reads*) 'The cook will be a better judge than the guest who is not a cook, of the pleasure to be derived from the dinner which is in preparation ...'

David: Well, he can't have visited many restaurants! Yesterday I ate at a French restaurant. The restaurant critics praised it, cooks at other restaurants praised it, it was even recommended in *Time* magazine and what happened? I almost threw up!

Charles: Precisely! And are the experts better 'in themselves'? No. They are treated better and paid better because lots of people believe in what they say. Because to many people it seems good to have an expert who tells them what to do.

Leslie: Well, it seems the 'real' criticisms are not much better than the sham criticisms.

Dr Cole: Wait a minute – we are not yet finished! I agree that some things Socrates says are not too convincing – but there are other arguments! For example Socrates argues that the principle of Protagoras refutes itself.

Jack: You are going to have a hard time with that one! Socrates calls it an 'exquisite' argument but all I see is a rather simple-minded swindle. Look at it. In 170 he quotes Protagoras, for he wants to refute him with his own words. He quotes him as saying that what seems to a man also is for him. And note, he does not say that what seems to a man is, but that what seems to a man is *for him*.

Dr Cole: Yes, that is what Protagoras says.

Jack: Now, if I understand the argument correctly he points out that lots of people don't share that belief. They don't say 'What seems to me, is for me', they disregard what seems to them, most of the time they don't even have an opinion of their own, they just follow an expert.

David: Well, it just seems to them that experts have the truth.

Jack: No, that's not the point I wanted to make. Confronted with Protagoras' dictum most people would say, according to Socrates, that they certainly are not measures, that experts alone are measures and the experts themselves would say, yes, we know what we are talking about, nobody else does. Is that not what Socrates says?

Dr Cole: Not in these words, but that is the sense.
Jack: And then, here towards the end, Socrates says this means that Protagoras himself, by his very principle, must admit that his principle is *false* – note, not false *for* these people, or false *for* these experts, as he ought to say according to the wording of the principle, but simply *false*. Well, I repeat, that is not an argument, that is a swindle.
Seidenberg: That can't possibly be the right interpretation! I don't say that Plato would never use tricks, but if he wanted to put one over on us, as you Americans say, he would not do it in such a simple-minded manner. Look! When he first introduces Protagoras' principle he is very careful to add the 'for him', also in the examples which he gives: the wind is cold *for him* who feels cold, not cold *for him* who feels warm . . . and so on. The same is true of the passage we are discussing now. It starts out with: what appears to a man, is *for him*. So, if he drops the 'for him', he must have a reason for doing so.
Jack: I wish I knew what it is.
Seidenberg: Well, let me try. (*To Jack*) I don't have your logical education and I may make mistakes, but I'll try. So. Protagoras says 'What seems to a man is for him' or, with a simple change, 'What seems to a man is true for him'. Also, 'What seems that it is not for a man is not true for that man'. Do you agree?
Jack: Yes, go on.
Seidenberg: And we can further say, taking those two things together, that Protagoras pronounces the *equivalence* of 'It seems to x that p' and 'It is true for x that p'. Am I right so far?
Dr Cole: I would say, yes.
Seidenberg: Now I want to imitate you logicians (*to Jack*) – I call this equivalence P. Now assume that somebody denies P. Socrates, for example.
Jack: Well, then it seems to him that non-P and, therefore, for him, non-P, in agreement with the principle.
Seidenberg: That may be. He may say 'non-P' in accordance with the principle – but saying it, no matter in accordance with what principle, he denies the principle. Note, he does not deny it universally. Socrates does not say 'For me P is never true', or 'For all propositions p and all people x it is false that if it seems to x that p then p is true for x' – he simply says 'For me P is false' which means that for him there are *some*

sentences where the *appearance*, for a person, that they are true does not make them *true* for that person. Socrates certainly would not deny P for sense-data statements – here to appear true is indeed to be true, and he says so himself.
Jack: And?
Seidenberg: Well, according to Protagoras what appears to a person is for that person. So according to Protagoras some appearances (for Socrates) differ from the corresponding truths (for Socrates). And so, according to Protagoras P is not true – for him, for Protagoras himself. The only way he could get out of trouble would be by denying that two people can ever have opinions about the same sentence, but in this case his principle which is supposed to be about any proposition held by any person and not only about propositions held by Protagoras ceases to be meaningful. Now it is true that Plato expresses the matter by saying that the principle is false – period; but he can do this, for once 'true for' has been separated from 'seem to', there is no further reason for retaining the 'for', because it entered only in analogy to the seeming. So for me the argument is really decisive.
Bruce: Well, I am not so convinced. I don't say that your interpretation of the argument was not correct, but you both, Plato and you, made one big assumption. You assumed that a principle, or a procedure which, applied to itself, leads to an absurdity or a contradiction, has to be given up. That is a very questionable assumption. To start with, Protagoras may not have wanted to use his principle in this way.
Dr Cole: I am not so sure. Protagoras was a sophist and sophists were artisans in the construction of tricky arguments.
Charles: Then let us separate Protagoras' principle from his interpretation of it. What can we do with the principle? Must we accept the refutation we have just heard?
Bruce: No, because we need not accept the rule that a principle whose self-application creates trouble must be given up. Look at the sentence in the space below:

the only sentence in this space in false

Reading the sentence I can infer that it is true, and if true then false and if false then true – and so on. It is the old paradox of the liar all over again. Some people concluded that self-reference has to be avoided; a sentence must *never* talk about itself. For example, I must never utter a sentence like 'I am now talking very softly'. Why? Because it was assumed that all the possible sentences of a language have already been pronounced and exist as an abstract system. Introducing self-reference into such a system creates trouble, naturally. But the languages we speak are not such systems. Their sentences do not already exist, they are produced, one by one, as we speak, and rules of speaking take shape accordingly. Assume I say 'Pink melancholy climbed over the hills'. Do I make sense? Not in a tyrannical system where colour words are supposed to be applied to material objects only. Still, I may be introducing a new poetic fashion, I may utter the statement to convey the mood of a dream to my psychiatrist – and he most likely will understand what I mean – I may say it to a singing student to help her placing her voice – and believe me, singing teachers do use statements like these, and with great success! In each of these cases we not only follow rules but constitute and modify them by the way in which we proceed.

Gaetano: That is very interesting. I am now studying the theory of harmony and composition. Well, there are teachers who lay down rules, give some abstract reasons for them and insist that everybody follow the rules. Turning to history they find lots of exceptions. Composers constantly violate the rules. What do these teachers do? They either criticize the composers, or they make the rules more and more complicated. Walter Piston, in his theory of harmony, goes a different way. I'll never forget one of the sentences where he formulates his attitude. 'Music', he says, 'is the result of composition, not of the application of rules.' Now you say that language is the result of speaking, not of an application of rules; therefore, one cannot judge a language by what happens when one freezes part of it and puts it into a computer.

Arthur: And I would add that science is the result of doing research, not of following rules, and therefore one cannot judge science by abstract epistemological rules except when these rules are a result of a special and constantly changing epistemological *practice*.

Jack: But what becomes now of proofs, such as Goedel's incompleteness proof? Or of the much simpler proof of the consistency of the propositional calculus?

Gaetano: I have thought about that. This proof is not about spoken languages, for example about languages using numbers, but about formal reconstructions of them and it shows that such reconstructions are definitely limited. If you decide to stick to certain rules, come what may, then you are bound to run into all sorts of obstacles.
Bruce: These are excellent illustrations of what I wanted to say! Applying the attitude of a composer, or of a speaker of a language to Protagoras' principle, we regard it as a rule of thumb whose meaning emerges from its use and is not fixed in advance. Socrates' arguments, therefore, do not refute relativism. They refute a Platonic version of relativism where statements are not tied to utterances but exist independently of speech so that a new statement may turn the preceding performance into a farce.
Jack: Well, if you decide to make up your statements as you go along then, of course, nobody can refute you.
Arthur: Not at all! The complex of statements called 'Newton's theory' changed in the hands of Euler, the Bernoullis, Lagrange and Hamilton; in a way it was the same theory, in a way it was not, and yet scientists eventually specified definite troubles for this not very stable structure. If you adopt Bruce's practical attitude then your ideas about the relation between a theory and its difficulties will of course have to be modified. You will no longer think of a theory as a well-defined entity that says exactly what difficulties will make it disappear; you will think of it as a vague promise whose meaning is constantly being changed and refined by the difficulties one decides to accept. We already talked about this a little earlier when discussing 'All ravens are black' and Socrates' rejection of his own first series of criticisms. In a way logicians and the philosophers who follow their lead are very superficial. They see a statement, such as Protagoras' statement. They interpret the statement in a simple-minded way and they triumphantly refute it! But this procedure would have killed science long ago. Every scientific theory, interpreted in a literal way, is in conflict with numerous facts! Plato was aware of this situation, he criticized the practice of easy removal, but then fell for it and used it himself.
Charles: Which means that we must separate relativism from what Socrates makes of it for the purpose of easy refutation ...

Leslie: And from what Protagoras may have made of it, assuming he treated the statement in the manner of a logician.
Bruce: Correct. Now in discussing relativism I think it is good to start with some practical matters. What are our intentions? I would say the intentions of a relativist are to protect individuals, groups, cultures from the actions of those who think they have found truth. And here I would like to emphasize two things. First, tolerance. Not the kind of tolerance that says 'Well, those fools don't know anything – but they have a right to live as they see fit – so, let us leave them alone'. That would be a rather contemptible kind of tolerance, if you ask me. No, the tolerance of the relativist assumes that the people tolerated have achievements of their own and have survived because of these achievements. It is not easy to explain what the achievements consist in. We certainly cannot speak of 'systems of thought' or 'systems of living' – the absurdity of such an assumption became very clear in our debate. But we can isolate, approximately, a particular stage of one culture and compare it with a particular stage of another and different culture and come to the conclusion that a more or less agreeable life is possible in both. Of course, a member of culture P may feel very uncomfortable in culture Q, but that is not the point. The point is that the people who grew up in Q and come to know P may find advantages and drawbacks and in the end may prefer P to their own way of life – and they may have excellent reasons for their choice. In such circumstances a statement like 'But he chose falsehood over truth' is just empty talk.
Arnold: I cannot agree with this! Take any statement, well, it is either true or false, no matter what people think about it. I agree that the wicked may be happy and the just miserable – but that does not make the wicked just.
Charles: You would be right if the world were the same in all its parts and did not change in accordance with the way in which people behave. Then you could really say, yes, I have here a statement, which is one stable entity, and there a world, which is another stable entity, there exists a certain objective relation between the two, the one either 'fits' or does not 'fit' the other, though I may never know what is actually the case. But assume that the world or, to use a more general term,

Being, reacts to the way in which you behave, or in which a whole tradition behaves, that it reacts differently to different approaches and that there is no way of connecting the reactions with a universal substance or with universal laws. Assume also that Being reacts positively, i.e. life-sustaining and truth-confirming to more than one approach, then all we can say is that *being approached scientifically* Being gives us, one after another, a closed world, an eternal and infinite universe, a big bang, a great wall of galaxies and, in the small, an unchanging Parmenidean block, Democritean atoms and so on until we have quarks etc., and that *being approached 'spiritually'* it gives us gods, not just ideas of them, but real visible gods whose actions can be followed in detail – and life is sustained in all these circumstances. Well, in such a world you *cannot* say that the gods are illusions – they are really there, though not absolutely, but in response to special kinds of actions, and you *cannot* say that everything obeys and always has obeyed the laws of quantum mechanics, for these laws, too, turn up only after you have moved through a complex historical development; what you *can* say is that different cultures and different historical trends (in the approximate and restricted sense introduced earlier) have a foundation in reality and that knowledge is 'relative' in that sense.
Lee Feng: Are you saying that man and entire cultures are measures, but that Being is also a measure and that whatever world we live in is a result of these two measures interacting?
Charles: Yes; this is an excellent formulation. Many people make the mistake of assuming that the world that arose as a response to their actions, or their history, underlies all other cultures, only the others are too stupid to notice it. But there is no way to discover the mechanism according to which the various worlds emerge from Being.
Lee Feng: I am not too happy about this last assumption – why should it not be possible one fine day to discover such a mechanism?
Charles: Because discoveries are historical events – they cannot be foreseen. Knowing the mechanism of interaction we might be able to foresee them – hence no such mechanisms will ever be known. Expressed differently we might say that Nature's actions cannot be foreseen by a creature whose life is

stretched out in time. Such a creature can foresee what happens *within* a particular world, it cannot foresee the change from one world to another.
Jack: I want to come back to Lee Feng's uneasiness – why it should not be possible to discover the laws of Being itself. It is easy to give models of situations showing limits of knowledge, even according to the laws of our own limited universe. For example, the pure quantum state of the table before me. To find it I would have to have a measuring device larger than the entire universe and if I had it, it would blow up the table, not measure it. Interpreting our brain as a computer we can make some assumptions about its capacity – and then certain things would be beyond our comprehension – according to facts and laws we know and accept. So why should Being not react to human actions with worlds that are at least partially comprehensible to humans while remaining incomprehensible itself?
Arnold: You almost speak as if Being were a person.
Charles: It may well be – as a matter of fact I would not at all be averse to thinking of it as a kind of *deus-sive-natura*, only without the Spinozan constipation.
Jack: So relativism now amounts to saying that there is not one stable nature but an indeterminate reality, unknowable in principle, which may reject certain approaches – some actions remain without response – but leaves much more leeway than is assumed by realists such as Plato or Einstein?
Charles: I think so. There are different cultures, and they are not at all composed of lunatics, nor do they work because of an extreme version of Protagoras' principle, but because Being permits different approaches and encourages a practical relativism – within certain limits: man, or certain temporarily stable aspects of cultures are measures of things *to the extent to which Being permits them to be measures*. Moreover, Being permits individuals or cultures the amount of independence that is needed to be a measure in this restricted sense. A single individual, starting out on a lonely path, may 'touch a nerve' of Being and provide a stimulus for an entirely new world. We simply cannot separate the discussion of relativism and tolerance from cosmology, or even theology – a purely logical discussion is not only naive, it does not even make sense.
Dr Cole: Well, Plato seems to be of the same opinion for later

on, in the *Timaeus,* he builds up a whole cosmology as a background to explaining knowledge ...
(Learned-looking individual appears at the door): I am sorry, I have to start my class now ...
Dr Cole (looking at his watch): Already? We have barely covered half of the dialogue.
Donald (in a plaintive voice): What is the result?
Charles: You mean you haven't learned anything?
Donald: No – I tried to make some notes, but you jumped around from one topic to another, it was complete chaos ...
Charles: You mean to say a result is something you can write down?
Donald: What else?
Seidenberg (trying to mediate): But look, remember when we talked about Plato's style and why he opposed the scholarly essay ...
Donald: You mean everything is supposed to be up in the air?
Charles: Not up in the air, but not on paper either – in the mind, as a memory and an attitude.
Donald: That is not what I mean by philosophy ...
(The learned-looking individual): You are philosophers? No wonder you can't finish in time ...
Grazia (appears at the doorway – an attractive lady with curly hair and a heavy Italian accent): Is this the class on the theory of knowledge?
Dr Cole (looking interested): It was, I am sorry; it is over.
Grazia (disappointed): Why am I always late!
Dr Cole (softly): Actually, you did not miss very much.
Grazia: Aren't you the teacher?
Dr Cole (embarrassed): Yes, but I don't want to be a tyrant ...
Grazia: You let people talk? There was a discussion? I might have been able to say something?
Dr Cole: If you could have stopped the others.
Grazia (with a superior look): Weeeell, I don't think that would have been a problem. I am really sorry I missed that seminar ...
(Grazia disappears with Dr Cole, talking animatedly. Everybody is gone. Donald alone remains, mumbling): That was my last philosophy class. I'll never get a grade in this way.

[illegible]
[illegible]
[illegible]
[illegible]
[illegible]
[illegible]
[illegible]
[illegible]
[illegible]
[illegible]
[illegible] What else?
[illegible]
[illegible]
[illegible]
[illegible] Yes indeed, every man is supposed to [illegible]
[illegible]
[illegible]
[illegible]
[illegible]
[illegible]
[illegible]
[illegible]
[illegible]
[illegible]
[illegible]
[illegible] And I'm in the wrong?
[illegible] You see? I didn't want to be a [illegible]
[illegible]
[illegible]
[illegible]
[illegible]
[illegible]
[illegible]
[illegible]

Second Dialogue (*1976*)

Second Dialogue

The free man always has time at his disposal to converse in peace at his leisure. He will pass, as we shall in our dialogue, from one argument to another; like us he will leave the old for a fresh one which takes his fancy more; and he does not care how long and how short the discussion may be, if only it attains the truth. The professional, or the expert, on the other hand, is always talking against time, hurried on by the clock; there is no space to enlarge on any subject he chooses, but the adversary, or his editor stands over him ready to recite a schedule of the points to which he must confine himself. He is a slave disputing about a fellow slave before a master sitting in judgement with some definite plea in his hand; and the issue is never indifferent, but his personal concerns are always at stake, sometimes even his salary. Hence he acquires a tense and bitter shrewdness ...

After Plato, Theaetetus

A: What have you got against critical rationalism?
B: Critical rationalism?
A: Yes, critical rationalism; Popper's philosophy.
B: I didn't know Popper had a philosophy.
A: You cannot be serious. You were his student ...
B: I listened to some of his lectures ...
A: And became his pupil ...
B: I know this is what Popperians say ...

A: You translated Popper's *Open Society* ...
B: I needed the money ...
A: You mentioned Popper in footnotes, and quite frequently ...
B: Because he, and his pupils begged me to do so and I am kindhearted. Little did I know that one fine day such friendly gestures would give rise to serious dissertations about 'influences'.
A: But you were a 'Popperian' – all your arguments were in the Popperian style.
B: That is is where you are mistaken. It is quite true that some of my discussions with Popper are reflected in my early writings – but so are my discussions with Anscombe, Wittgenstein, Hollitscher, Bohr, and even my reading of Dadaism, Expressionism, Nazi authorities has left a trace here and there. You see, when I come across some unusual ideas I try them out. And my way of trying them out is to push them to the extreme. There is not a single idea, however absurd and repulsive, that has not a sensible aspect and there is not a single view, however plausible and humanitarian, that does not encourage and then conceal our stupidity and our criminal tendencies. There is much Wittgenstein in all my papers – but Wittgensteinians neither seek nor are in need of great numbers of followers and so they do not claim me as one of their own. Besides they understand that while I regard Wittgenstein as one of the great philosophers of the twentieth century ...
A: Greater than Popper?
B: Popper is not a philosopher, he is a pedant – this is why the Germans love him so. At any rate – the Wittgensteinians realize that my admiration for Wittgenstein does not yet make me a Wittgensteinian. But this is all beside the point ...
A: Not quite. For what you claim is that while you may *use* certain ideas you need not *accept* them.
B: Yes.
A: Are you an anarchist?
B: I don't know – I haven't considered the matter.
A: But you have written a book on anarchism!
B: And?
A: Don't you want to be taken seriously?
B: What has that got to do with it?
A: I do not understand you.

B: When a good play is performed the audience takes the action and the speeches of the actors very seriously; they identify now with the one, now with the other character and they do so even though they know that the actor playing the puritan is a rake in his private life and the bomb-throwing anarchist a frightened mouse.
A: But they take the writer seriously!
B: No, they don't! When the play gets hold of them they feel constrained to consider problems they never thought about no matter what additional information they may obtain when the play is over. And this additional information is not really relevant ...
A: But assume the writer produced a clever hoax ...
B: What do you mean – hoax? He wrote a play – didn't he? The play had some effect, didn't it? It made people think – didn't it?
A: It made them think by deceiving them.
B: They were not deceived for they did not think about the author. And if it turns out that his beliefs are different from those of his characters then we shall admire him even more for being able to transcend the narrow boundaries of his private life. You seem to prefer a playwright who is a preacher ...
A: I prefer a playwright I can *trust* ...
B: Because you don't want to think! You want *him* to assume responsibility for his ideas so that you can accept them without qualms and without having to examine them in detail. But let me assure you that his being honest would not help you. There are many honest morons, and criminals.
A: Are you against honesty?
B: I cannot answer a question like this.
A: Many people can.
B: Again, because they don't think. The situations in which we are involved and about which we are supposed to be 'honest' can be described in many different ways. Having been described they are not the same as before. Wanting to be 'honest' I may say 'I love Maureen' and I say it because I want to be honest. But having said it I start having doubts – to say that I 'love' her is saying a little too much. 'I like Maureen' is better. But it is not perfect. Something is missing – and so on. I do not encounter these troubles when simply telling the story

of my affair with Maureen – of course I love her – what else? But the request to be honest throws a peculiar light over my story, it becomes ambiguous ...

A: Now you say that you not only don't know what honesty is, you also don't know what love is.

B: But I don't.

A: Don't you think you are a little peculiar? People know well enough if they love their wives, their parents ...

B: They are ready to say 'I love you' at the drop of a hat – I admit that. But do they know? A little baby says 'I love you' to its mother. The one member of a sado-masochistic relationship says 'I love you' to the other while being whipped – think of Liliana Cavani's *Night Porter*. The words come without effort – but do they mean the same thing?

A: Well, going on like this you will soon say that we never know what we are doing and that our whole life is a chimaera ...

B: And what if it is? At any rate – whatever solidity there seems to be in what we say is the result of thoughtlessness, and the theatre is a most appropriate instrument of communication because it both appeals to this thoughtlessness and makes it explicit. But back to honesty – assume I know what it is and assume it implies that I should not lie. Then very often my wish to be honest will be in conflict with my wish to be kind.

A: Kant has a reply to that. Being dishonest to one particular person injures all of humanity because humanity is based on trust. The smallest lie told in the world violates this trust and injures humanity.

B: Well, here is one of the reasons why I so often have a feeling of contempt for philosophers ...

A: But you are a philosopher yourself!

B: No, I am not! I am a professor of philosophy, which means a civil servant. But back to Kant! He constructs a caricature, a monstrous caricature of what it means to be human, and uses it as a justification for being cruel without any feeling of regrets, no, quite the contrary, with the wonderful feeling of having done 'the right thing'. Philosophers are great artists in finding wonderful reasons for cruel actions ...

A: Please stop – I can well do without your speeches!

B: No, listen. Before me is a dying woman. All her happiness is centred in her son. She has great pains. She knows she is going to die. She asks 'What is Arthur doing?' Now Arthur is in prison. Shall I tell her that and make her leave this world in despair, or shall I tell her 'Arthur is OK'? Now Kant says that her despair does not count when compared with the well-being of humanity. But this 'well-being' is entirely a monster of his own construction. Not a single suffering person in Ethiopia will feel elated, or suffer less, because I have been cruel to the woman before me. And these are the things that count, not the ravings of a philosophical Dr Mabuse.

A: Now if that is your attitude – does it mean that you are against making the idea of honesty an important part of our behaviour and, therefore, of our education?

B: Well, if *that* was the question, then my answer is obvious. It should be an important part of our education *provided* we are also told that it has limits and receive some instruction as to how to behave in these limits.

A: Would you say the same about truth and decency?

B: I would say the same about all ideas expressed by Big Words such as Truth, Honesty, Justice which batter our brains and mutilate our best instincts.

A: So for you education is a way of protecting people from being educated.

B: Precisely. You know Bela Lugosi?

A: Yes, of course.

B: He played Dracula.

A: He played it very well.

B: Rumour has it he slept in a coffin.

A: Is this not going a little too far?

B: Why?

A: There is more to life than playing Dracula.

B: Precisely! And there is much more to life than is contained in any particular creed, philosophy, point of view, form of life or what have you and so you should never be trained to sleep in the coffin of a particular set of ideas day and night and an author who presents a view to his readers should never be so shortsighted as to believe that there is nothing more to be said.

A: There is more to life than truth, honesty ...

B: Good lord, when will you stop singing those silly arias which have no cognitive content whatsoever and just function

like dogs' whistles: they put the faithful into a state of agressive readiness – excepting their brains of course. Give me any series of virtues and there is another virtue that might on occasions conflict with it. Charity might conflict with justice and truthfulness, love with justice and again truthfulness, honesty with the wish to preserve somebody's life and so on. Moreover, we never know all the virtues that might give content to our lives, we have just started thinking on these matters and so any eternal principle we may want to defend today will most likely be overruled tomorrow unless we get brainwashed to such an extent that we cease to be human beings and become truth-machines and honesty-computers. There is indeed much more to life than truth and honesty. People must be able to see this richness, they must learn how to deal with it, which means they must receive an education that contains more than just a few barren precepts or, to express it negatively, they must be protected from those who want them to become faithful copies of their own mental squalor.
A: So you really are against education.
B: On the contrary! I regard education – the right kind of education – as a most necessary aid to life. I think the poor creatures who were sent into the world just because a man or a woman were bored with each other, felt lonely and hoped that producing a nice little pet might improve matters, or because mama forgot to insert her intra-uterine device, or because mama and papa were Catholics and did not dare to have pleasure without procreation – I think these poor creatures need some protection. They got life without having asked for it – and yet from the very first day of their existence they are pushed around, forbidden to do this, ordered to do that, any conceivable pressure is exerted upon them including the inhumane pressure deriving from the need for love and sympathy. So they grow up. They become 'responsible'. And now the pressures are refined. Instead of the whip we have the argument, instead of parental threats the pressures issuing from some midget whom his fellow midgets regard as a 'great man'. Instead of eating his supper he is supposed to search for truth. But why should the children of tomorrow have to imitate the leading idiots of today? Why should those upon whom we have imposed existence not view this existence in their own terms? Don't they have a right to lead their own lives? Don't they have a right to please themselves even if this

scares the beejesus out of their teachers, fathers, mothers as well as of the local police force? Why should they not decide against Reason and Truth ...
A: You must be dreaming ...
B: And this is my good right. This is everybody's good right and it must not be taken from us by an education that maims instead of helping us to develop our own being to the fullest.
A: 'Develop our own being to the fullest' – you are the most egotistical man I have ever met.
B: I didn't say I want this for myself. I am too old to make use of the freedom I think should be given to everyone and too loused up by a chaotic and ill-arranged life. But I say that anybody who has been put into this world without having been asked can laugh into the face of anyone who wants to inform him about 'duties', 'obligations' and what have you. I didn't ask to be born. I didn't beg my mother to hop into bed with papa so that I might see the light of day. I didn't beg my parents to take care of me and my teachers to instruct me and so I owe them nothing. Nor do I owe anything to the 'leaders of mankind' and nobody can expect me to take seriously the silly games they invented to keep themselves amused ...
A: Christ did not preach to keep himself amused ...
B: In a way he did – he certainly did not act contrary to his wishes. He envisaged a certain form of life, he wanted to spread it, after some hesitation he even tried to *force* people to pay attention to him. He set in motion a historical process in the course of which millions of people were tortured, maimed, little children were burned because some inquisitor felt 'responsible' for their souls....
A: You cannot blame the inquisition on Christ!
B: But I can! Any teacher who wants to introduce new ideas, a new form of life must realize two things. First that ideas will be misused unless they have some inbuilt protection. Voltaire's ideas had this protection, Nietzsche's ideas had not. Nietzsche was used by the Nazis, Voltaire was not. Secondly he must realize that a 'message' that helps in some circumstances may be deadly in others ...
A: What about the message that we should search for truth?
B: It makes us forget that a life without mystery is barren and that some things, for example our friends, should be loved rather than understood completely.
A: But there will always be things we do not know ...

B: I am thinking about things we should leave alone even if a search for truth seems to promise some results ...
A: This is sheer obscurantism ...
B: Yes, and I am in favour of being more obscurantist than anyone today dares to be.
A: But what is the advantage?
B: Have you ever been in love?
A: I think so ...
B: You think so.
A: Well, I think, I was.
B: Did you like it?
A: Did I like what?
B: Being in love?
A: Yes I liked it.
B: Did you try to examine why?
A: Yes, of course I did!
B: How did you proceed?
A: I asked questions.
B: Whom did you ask?
A: I asked some of my acquaintances. I also asked the lady in question.
B: How did she react?
A: She was very patient –
B: But she cooled off?
A: Yes, she did. She also told me that I had no business talking about her affairs with strangers.
B: Your search for truth conflicted with her request for privacy.
A: Apparently it did.
B: After your inquiries – did you love her more or less?
A: Well ...
B: The whole affair stopped.
A: Yes.
B: You killed it by your inquisitiveness.
A: But ...
B: But there is an area in every human being which you must respect, which you must not try to penetrate except when permitted to do so ...
A: I admit all this – but this is a very special case.
B: It is not – have a look at this book here.
A: *Human Guinea Pigs* – what is it about?

B: It is about truth-seeking doctors.
A: Well, doctors have to find means to cure patients.
B: At the patients' expense?
A: How else can they improve medicine?
B: Physics is based on experiment – isn't it?
A: Yes.
B: The best results are those obtained in a laboratory.
A: Yes.
B: But the stars are too big and too far away to carry out laboratory experiments with them.
A: Agreed.
B: Therefore one had to find different methods to obtain knowledge about them. And astronomy flourished long before physics despite the absence of laboratory results.
A: But patients are available, lots of them.
B: No, they are not. Their bodies are their own and no doctor has the right to dig into them just to satisfy his curiosity.
A: How then is he supposed to heal?
B: By devising a kind of medicine that does not rely on interference with the human body.
A: But such a medicine is impossible.
B: It is not only not impossible, it exists. The so-called empiricist schools in medicine have assembled detailed information about changes in patients that can be observed without interference – changes in the colour of the eyes, texture and colour of skin, muscle tonus, consistency of stool, urine, spittle, texture of the mucous membranes, reflexes.
A: It is hardly possible to base diagnosis and therapy on these.
B: That just shows how little you know about medicine and the art of healing. Pulse diagnosis is very effective to find subtle disturbances of the organism that do not show on any 'scientific' test, they diagnose the usual illnesses without the expensive machinery modern medicine relies on, X-rays become unnecessary and so do other dangerous diagnostic procedures.
A: Well, it is possible perhaps to find some correlations – but we can hardly say that they lead to an understanding of illness.
B: But understanding is not what is required from a physician. He has to heal . . .
A: But he must also proceed in a scientific manner.

B: Why should he? As a matter of fact one can easily show that 'proceeding in a scientific way' with content increase and all that jazz often *conflicts* with the task of healing.
A: What paradox are you going to concoct now?
B: No paradox at all! You admit that philosophers have often produced ideas that were regarded as senseless drivel by the common folk?
A: I admit that.
B: On the other hand there are people whose behaviour looks like madness to us but who have important functions in societies different from our own?
A: What do you have in mind?
B: Prophets, shamans. New Yorkers today would regard a genuine Hebrew prophet as a madman even if he spoke the most beautiful Brooklynese.
A: And rightly so, for the situation has changed since Nebuchadnezzar, or Herod.
B: Not so fast! Do you know that some people are of great help to their relatives, they are loved by them, they inspire them, though the rest of the village or the city would rather be without them?
A: I don't know anyone like that – but I can well imagine such a situation.
B: Old people today are mostly regarded as medical problems – they are moved off to some nursery home, or some hospital for the aged . . .
A: . . . because they need care, because they cannot take care of themselves.
B: No, because there is nothing for them to do. In the USA today ageing people are just human waste and, naturally, they soon behave like it. There are other societies where responsibilities increase with age, where what we today call senile babbling is regarded as worthy of attention, where the young learn from the experience of their ancestors . . .
A: . . . we have historians for that.
B: And what do these historians do? They get grants to concoct oral histories, which means histories as reported by the survivors of events long gone by. It would be better to listen to these reports directly, without the filter of an intellectual being interposed between the source and those who can learn

from it. Do you know that the attitude of people towards children changed considerably in the past two hundred years? Today we are very sentimental about children – but only a short time ago the death of a child meant no more than the death of a household pet. Even Rousseau, otherwise a very emotional man, wrote without much emotion about having sent his five children to an orphanage. No doubt you have also read Foucault's book on the change of attitude towards mental health, prison, crime. Some time ago the mentally ill were classified with the poor, or with people loath of work, before that mental aberrations were interpreted as results of a pact with the devil; today medicine has taken over ...

A: I have heard of all those things, though only vaguely and through rumour. But tell me, what has all this got to do with your promise ...

B: ... namely to show that scientific medicine may come into conflict with the wish to heal? Well, just as the idea of childhood, of death, of madness, of crime, the idea of a prison, the attitude toward the aged is different in different societies, even in different parts of one and the same society, just as it changes from one generation to the next, in the very same way the idea of health also changes.

A: Yes, I can see that. And I add that today we have to look to science for a proper definition of health.

B: For you a physician seems to be a kind of Dr Frankenstein. He finds an organism, says 'no good' and tries to rebuild it until it fits his idea of a healthy being.

A: Well, the patient hardly knows when he is sick and when he is not – extreme cases perhaps excepted.

B: He may not know when he is sick in the sense of some scientists, but he sure knows what kind of life he prefers and what kind of life he abhors.

A: You are an optimist.

B: Assume I am – does this mean that we should let somebody else decide for him?

A: Well, obviously, if he doesn't know somebody else has to make the decision.

B: That is not the only possibility.

A: What do you have in mind?

B: Education.

A: But that amounts to the same – we train a person to make the decisions the experts might make under the circumstances in question.
B: So education for you means turning people into experts.
A: Yes. Or at least giving them some understanding of expert knowledge.
B: Such as knowledge in astrology? Or acupuncture?
A: Of course not.
B: Why not?
A: Do I have to explain such trivial matters to you?
B: I wish you would.
A: Nobody takes astrology seriously.
B: I am sorry to contradict you – a lot of people take it seriously.
A: Nobody who has an inkling of science takes it seriously.
B: Of course not – science is now our favourite religion.
A: Do you seriously want to defend astrology?
B: Why not if the attacks are incompetent?
A: Are there not more important things?
B: Nothing is more important than to prevent people from being intimidated by ignorant bullies. Also astrology is an excellent example of the way in which the ignorant – i.e. scientists – joining hands with ignoramuses – philosophers of science, for example – have succeeded in deceiving everybody.
A: I can't believe my ears. There you sit and talk as if astrology were not complete nonsense. I don't see why we should waste any more time on this topic.
B: I shall agree with you as soon as you have convinced me that the matter is indeed a waste of time.
A (*sighing*): – OK, if you must play games. Astrology assumes a central symmetrical universe with the earth at the centre. That idea was given up with Copernicus. Astrologists have not taken this into account; they are scientific illiterates who perpetuate their dismal superstition without regard to the forward march of science, they rob people of money, replace responsible decisions by superficial predictions and so rob man of his free will, his most cherished possession!
B: Good lord – you rationalists really become poets when attacking false gods!
A: Poetry or not – I am right, so can we now return to this matter of medicine?

B: Not yet.
A (*desperate*): Another diversion!
B: No diversion, only a simple remark. Did you know that the objection from free will . . .
A: . . . a very important objection!
B: And also the objection from the fate of twins . . .
A: . . . another excellent objection!
B: . . . were both made by the church fathers, for example by St Augustine?
A: No, I did not know that – but what does it matter?
B: What matters is that the battle against astrologists was not started by scientists but by the church, and for religious reasons. And I think that the violence which characterizes the battle today is still a hangover from medieval times, however 'scientific' its main proponents pretend to be.
A: That is quite interesting . . .
B: . . . and important for it shows that scientists, despite their protestations to the contrary, have taken over some important attitudes of the church.
A: I cannot comment on that. It is interesting, but not relevant for what counts are arguments, not influences.
B: Have you heard of Kepler?
A (*looking offended*): Of course I have.
B: Did you know he wrote horoscopes?
A: Because he had to earn a living!
B: That he also wrote essays defending astrology?
A: He can hardly have been serious.
B: Why not?
A: One of the foremost Copernican astronomers?
B: Yes, and he not only defended astrology and practised it, he also revised it and accumulated evidence for his revised version.
A (*looks unhappy*).
B: You don't have to believe me. Here, read Kepler himself, his *Tertius Interveniens* and other essays in the *Collected Works*, read Norbert Herz's old essay on Kepler's astrology . . .
A: Well, in some way I can understand the matter – after all, the physics of the time was not very advanced.
B: But that was not your argument! You said that astrology was turned into nonsense by the new *astronomy*. Now, we have here a new astronomer, one of the best new astronomers in

fact, and he writes a defence of astrology. And he not only writes a defence, he collects evidence, he improves the subject ...

A: Maybe, I was a little hasty but, after all, to err is human ...

B: That was not your attitude at the beginning of your argument! You cursed the astrologists as if they were criminals, as if their trial had already been completed, and with the most condemning evidence against them. Now suddenly 'to err is human' – how tolerant you guys are towards your own mistakes!

A: OK, OK – I admit I was hasty in my judgement but, after all, astrology has so many weaknesses that the refutation of one argument against it does not improve the situation even if Kepler should once have decided to defend it. These were other times, science and superstition were not as clearly separated as they are today and the most outstanding scientists sometimes held absurd doctrines. Kepler defended astrology – admitted. That does not make it better. It is still a vile superstition.

B: And, pray, why?

A: To assume that the stars influence our lives ...

B: Is it not true that the Sun shines today?

A: And?

B: Is it not true that you wear a light shirt and not a pullover? And that your mood is better than it would be if it rained?

A: Now, you are getting absurd. Nobody denies that the Sun influences the weather.

B: And the Moon?

A: Definitely not.

B: What about the tides?

A: That is something different.

B: But Galileo, taking your position, denied that the tides had anything to do with the Moon – astrology is silly, therefore the tides must have a different cause. He was wrong.

A: Because a later theory that was well confirmed showed him to be wrong.

B: Which means that we cannot rest content with simply saying: 'The moon has no influence on the weather' – we must examine the matter.

A: Agreed.

B: And the same about the validity of horoscopes.
A: *That* is not necessary. Everybody knows that the forces of the stars are too weak to have such an influence.
B: Do you know what a plasma is?
A: A cloud of electrons?
B: Do you know that the Sun is surrounded by a huge plasma?
A: Yes, I have heard of it.
B: That the same is true of the planets?
A: That I did not know, but it seems entirely plausible.
B: These clouds interpenetrate and interact ...
A: Ah, magnetic storms and such things?
B: Yes. Now solar activity influences short-wave reception. Solar activity in turn depends on the relative position of the planetary plasmas which means it depends on the relative position of the planets. Thus one can predict certain peculiarities of short-wave reception from the position of the planets – there exists a radioastrology and it has been founded by researchers at RCA.
A: That has nothing whatever to do with astrology. Astrology deals with details in the lives of humans.
B: Not exclusively. It also deals with animals, clouds, storms, plants, with any kind of connection between the heavens and earth. But that was not your argument – your second argument. Your second argument was that the influences of the planets would be too weak to have noticeable effects on earth. And *that* argument is refuted by radioastrology.
A: I don't think this answer is completely fair. Of course – the planets influence the Sun, they influence each other and thereby also certain processes on Earth. They influence even people – after all, one can see them, talk about them, write poems about them. But these are not the influences I am now talking about. What I am talking about are influences which occur without our direct knowledge and which determine our actions in a subliminal manner. For example let us assume that I want to marry. I ask myself whether and why and what for. In the end I marry and think I have clear reasons. No, say the astrologists, you have omitted one important cause, namely the horoscope of your birth, or her birth, of your marriage and of the date when you first met. And this assertion, I think, is silly superstition.

B: What do you think of cancer research?
A: What do you mean?
B: Well, there exist many institutes dealing in cancer research. Do you think that the ideas that underlie their research are 'silly superstitions'?
A: Of course not!
B: And why not?
A: There has been progress.
B: Progress of what kind?
A: New theoretical insights.
B: But what about healing cancer?
A: There are operations, there is radiation treatment, chemical treatment ...
B: How did one treat cancer about thirty years ago?
A: Operations, I guess, surgical elimination of the cancerous tissue.
B: Have new methods of treatment been found?
A: Yes, as I said – radiation treatment ...
B: Which simply means eliminating the cancerous tissue in a more refined way. But we are still eliminating.
A: Yes.
B: Any radically different methods?
A: Not that I know of.
B: Now the methods of elimination existed already before microresearch and all the fine modern theories about cell structure started.
A: Yes.
B: Which means these theories so far have not led to any advance in treatment.
A: So you say.
B: It's not only what I say but what many responsible researchers say.
A: Who, for example?
B: Read the report by Daniel Greenberg in Vol. 4 (1974) of *Science and Government Reports,* or H. Oeser, *Krebsbekaempfung, Hoffnung und Realitaet.* Greenberg is particularly outspoken. He calls the American Cancer Society's proclamations that cancer is curable and that progress has been made 'reminiscent of Vietnam optimism prior to the deluge'. And yet we continue to support research and to regard it as scientific.
A: Of course.

B: The theoretical assumptions of cancer research are not condemned as silly superstitions.
A: Certainly not.
B: And why not?
A: Because there have been successes.
B: What kinds of successes?
A: We now understand much more about what goes on in a single cell.
B: But do we understand how cancer arises?
A: We do not – but we are on the way. Now what has all this got to do with astrology?
B: Quite a lot! I just told you about research that shows how the position of the planets can be correlated with short-wave reception on this earth.
A: And I replied that this does not make astrology a tiny bit less absurd.
B: You admit that it shows planetary influences upon terrestrial events.
A: Yes, but ...
B: The planets are not too weak to influence terrestrial events.
A: But it is not the kind of influence we are looking for.
B: It is precisely the type of unconscious influence you are looking for. Now you call cancer research scientific, you favour its continuation despite the distance that still remains. Why not apply the same courtesy to the basic assumptions of astrology?
A: Because in the case of astrology there is not only a distance between the results of research ...
B: ... which, as I said, are much more numerous than those I have produced so far ....
A: ... there is not only a distance between results of research and the theses under debate, there are also objections ...
B: ... such as the twin objection.
A: Such as the twin objection.
B: And you now suggest that a subject or a theory endangered by objections should be abolished, or regarded as unscientific.
A: A subject with *decisive* objections.
B: A subject with decisive objections should be abolished. That would be the end of cancer research!
A: Why?
B: More than thirty years of research and no decisive

advance. It would also have been the end of classical electromagnetism.

A: Why?

B: Because classical electromagnetism – the fundamental theory, that is – implies that there is no induced magnetism. Classical optics implied that looking at a picture situated at the focus of a lens you should see an infinitely deep hole and yet no such thing is ever seen. We have the infinities in quantum field theory ...

A: ... and we have renormalization ...

B: ... called a 'grotesque trick' by some physicists. Wherever you look you find theories beset by major difficulties – and yet they are retained because scientists have the pious faith that the difficulties may be solved one fine day. So why call this pious faith a 'plausible scientific assumption' when we are dealing with the quantum theory of fields and a 'silly and irresponsible superstition' in the case of astrology? Let us admit that research is often guided by hunches for which we have only little support and let us apply this admission equally to all subjects and not only to those scientists happen to favour for some religious reason!

A: But ...

B: I am not yet finished! You see, I would not at all object if the opponents of astrology were to say: we do not like astrology, we despise it, we shall never read books about it and we certainly shall not support it. This is quite legitimate. You can't force people to like what they hate, you can't even force them – and you *should not* force them – to inform themselves about the matter. But our scientists, our rational and objective scientists, do not just express their likes and dislikes, they act as if they had arguments and they use their considerable authority to give their dislikes force. But the arguments they actually use only show their pitiful illiteracy ...

A: OK, OK, I am sorry I ever brought the matter up – I hardly know anything about it ...

B: ... but you certainly acted as if you knew a lot when we began our little conversation. And the same is true of all scientists who make pronouncements about matters they have no idea about.

A: I doubt that there are many such scientists.

B: I am sorry to disillusion you. Just have a look at this paper.

It is the October/November number (1975) of the American journal *The Humanist* (strange title for what turns out to be a superchauvinistic rag). There is a series of articles criticizing astrology. The articles are badly written and full of mistakes. One of the authors says: 'Astrology was dealt a serious blow since it is a geocentric system'. This was your first argument. Incompetent, as we have seen. Another author writes that astrology originated from magic. But modern science also 'originated from magic' if one wants to talk in such a general fashion. Well, you might say, there are always scientists who overstep the boundaries of their competence and make fools of themselves. But now look at the end of the general statement that precedes the more detailed arguments. There are 186 signatures of scientists. 186 signatures! Quite obviously the learned gentlemen were not so much interested in convincing by argument as in pushing people around. For if you have one good argument – what is the use of that many signatures? What we have here is therefore nothing less than a scientific encyclical: the popes have have spoken, the matter is decided. Now look at the names! There are not just a few scientists from the backwoods – the foremost stars of the scientific establishment point their fingers at astrologers and curse them. John Eccles, the 'Popperian Knight', a Nobel Prize winner; Konrad Lorenz, the ethologist (and a man I greatly admire), a Nobel Prize winner; Crick, the co-discoverer of DNA, another Nobel-Bigshot – and so on and so forth. You have Samuelson, the economist, Pauling with two Nobel Prizes and his controversial (though quite reasonable) claim of the efficiency of large doses of vitamin C against colds and even cancer – everybody who is anybody in science lends his name to support a document that is a sink of ignorance and illiteracy. A few months after the document had appeared an interviewer from the BBC wanted to arrange a discussion between some of the Nobel Prize winners and defenders of astrology but all of the Nobel Prize winners declined – some with the remark that they had no idea about the details of astrology: the learned gentlemen did not know what they were talking about. Now such illiterates decide what is and what is not to be taught at our schools; such illiterates proclaim with supercilious contempt that old traditions which they have not studied and which they do not understand must be eradicated no matter how important they are to those who want to live in accordance with them; such illiterates interfere with our lives, at birth, when mothers are shipped off to hospitals so that their babies may at once become acquainted with the splendour of the faceless technological society they are going to inhabit; in early youth when talents are carefully determined and curricula carefully set up to get a maximum of the scientific religion into the adolescents' brain and so on till a 'mortuary science' finally takes care of the tired, worn-out and pollution-damaged body ...

A: Mortuary science?

B: Yes, a legitimate subject at many universities. Such illiterates also determine where and how we are going to use nuclear power, how our children are going to live, what is good medicine and what not, they waste millions of tax money on ridiculous projects and get up in arms when a better control of these moneys is suggested, these illiterates ...

A: Heaven help me – stop! How absurd can you get! You may be right about astrology – although I haven't yet conceded the matter ...

B: ... well, let us discuss it further.

A: No, no, no – no more astrology. I give in. I never said anything.

B: Accepted.

A: But these other topics you mention are not outside the scientists' competence, they are right in the centre of their competence – nuclear reactors, for example, or medicine, this is right in the centre of the competence of physicists and physicians or biologists. What you do is to infer incompetence in the expertise of these people from an alleged incompetence outside of it – a ridiculous inference!

B: OK – we need some more examples!

A: We'll never get anywhere in this way!

B: If by 'getting somewhere' you mean showing that science is king then of course I agree.

A: Well, what is this example of yours?

B: It is an example from archaeology. Some time ago it was discovered, by Thom, Hawkins, Marshack, Seidenberg and others that Stone Age man had a fairly highly developed astronomy and that megalithic structures such as Stonehenge were

astronomical observatories and computers for the prediction of important astronomical events ...
A: Such as?
B: Such as lunar eclipses, for example. These discoveries were made by a few men and rejected by the rest of the profession.
A: No doubt they had reasons.
B: Yes, they had reasons but listen to what kind of reasons they were. I have here the *Journal for the History of Astronomy* and an article by Professor Atkinson, the top expert on Stonehenge and similar structures. Now read what the learned gentleman says.
A (*reading*): 'Here, I incline, I am afraid, to a moderate pessimism if only because so many of us have been trained, like myself, in the humanities and thus lack the numeracy required ...'
B: Stop right here! Atkinson is 'pessimistic' about the results of those who assert the existence of a well developed Stone Age Astronomy because his training is incomplete. He does not know enough – and still tries to use his ignorance to throw doubt on unusual research procedures. This is one point I want to make. The second point is even more important. Atkinson lacks 'the numeracy required'. The builders of the megalithic sites he has studied his entire life had the 'numeracy' he says he 'lacks'. They were better informed than he and yet he and his fellow scientists for a considerable time used their own ignorance and the blank spaces it created in their minds to give low marks to the 'Stone Age Mind'. Many anthropologists being ignorant in the fields explored by 'primitive' tribes projected their own ignorance upon them and inferred a 'primitive mentality', producing 'superstitions' instead of 'scientific results'. Similarly many modern physicians being ignorant of the medicine of the *Nei Ching* sneer at acupuncture and try to have it banned by legal means. They use the law to exclude possible and fair tests. Now go on reading.
A: 'It is important that non-archaeologists should understand how disturbing to archaeologists are the implications of Thom's work ...' Who is Thom?
B: One of the researchers who has uncovered a rather complex

megalithic geometry, metrology, astronomy including knowledge even of the nutation of the Moon's path.
A: What is 'nutation'?
B: The Moon's trajectory is inclined to the ecliptic, about five degrees. The points of intersection between the path of the Moon and the ecliptic, the so-called nodes, move around the ecliptic in about 186 years. During that time the angle between the ecliptic and the path of the moon changes periodically and one of these changes is called the nutation. Its amplitude is about 9 minutes of arc and it was known to Stone Age astronomers. Go on reading.
A (*not quite understanding the explanation*): '... of Thom's work because they do not fit the conceptual model of the prehistory of Europe which has been current during the whole of the present century ...'
B: Well, that is said very clearly. Atkinson is 'disturbed' because a theory he is not equipped to understand does not suit him – but wait, now comes an even more interesting passage!
A: 'It is hardly surprising, therefore, that many prehistorians either ignore the implications of Thom's work, because they do not understand them, or resist them, because it is more comfortable to do so ...'
B: Well, here you have it black on white: new ideas are rejected 'because it is more comfortable to do so' – and that right in the centre of competence of the learned gentlemen. After that can one ever again trust a physician who says that a disfiguring and debilitating operation is the best way of rectifying a disease? After that, can one ever again trust a nuclear scientist who guarantees the safety of a proposed reactor? After that ...
A: I think you are making a mountain out of a molehill. Atkinson is a single case ...
B: But he makes us realize how 'the scientific mind' works and what obstacles it encounters. Take scientists in a certain area of research. They have basic assumptions which they hardly ever question, they have ways of viewing the evidence which they regard as the only natural procedures, and research consists in *using* the basic assumptions and methods, not in *examining* them. It is true the assumptions were once introduced to solve problems, or to remove difficulties, and that one knew then how to see them in perspective. But this time has long

gone by. Now one is not even aware of the assumptions made one defines research in their terms and regards research that proceeds in a different way as improper, unscientific and absurd. You say that scientists often make fools of themselves when pontificating outside the area of their competence but must be listened to when speaking about things they have studied in detail. Well, they never studied assumptions of the kind I just described and yet their research could not start without them. This means that *every part of science lies at its periphery and that expertise is never an argument.*

A: Can you give me an example of the assumptions you have in mind?

B: There are ideas about methodology, for example the idea that we must start with an experimental investigation, that we must not permit theoretical ideas to influence it, that we must base our theories on its results. Many statistical procedures in the social sciences are of this kind. Archaeology for a long time was the classification of implements without any assumptions about the minds of those who produced the implements. A 'culture' was not an organization of minds trying to solve certain problems, it was a collection of stones, scratchings and so on. Then there is the assumption that lack of repeatability of experiments cannot be due to extra-terrestrial influences. Michael Polanyi has described a variety of chemical reactions with well-defined results, the results were repeated in other laboratories, photographs were made, dissertations written, but one fine day the effect disappeared and was never seen again. Many chemists regarded this as an oddity – but they would not have looked for extra-terrestrial causes. This, to them, would have been sheer superstition.

A: They may have had reasons for their attitude.

B: Reasons as excellent as the reasons against astrology I have just discussed – incompetent and ridiculous reasons. Then there is the belief that scientific research not clinical experience leads to better methods of healing. Closely connected with this belief is the idea that every illness has a proximate cause which is highly theoretical and which must be found. Diagnosis is supposed to find this proximate cause – this is why we have X-ray diagnosis, exploratory surgery, biopsies and similar procedures.

A: Well, how else are you going to find out what is going on?

B: For example by inspecting pulse, urine, texture of skin . . .
A: In this manner you will never find the particular disturbance that caused the illness.
B: But who says that an illness is caused by an event that can be localized? Illness may be a structural modification of the life-process that has no localizable cause though it involves many localizable changes and the best diagnosis might come from attending to overall changes of the body such as weight, pulse, muscle tone and so on.
A: We know better than that. Microbiology . . .
B: Microbiology deals with localizable events and omits the very processes I am talking about.
A: But the human body and the life process are constituted by microbiological processes.
B: This is a hypothesis that has been quite successful in a certain domain – but who says that it will continue to be successful outside this domain? Besides, molecular biological results are results one gets by following a line of least resistance. Complex problems are simply pushed aside.
A: We have to find out!
B: At the expense of the patient?
A: What do you mean?
B: Well, obviously the efficiency of your medicine will depend on the adequacy of your assumptions. Trying to push inadequate assumptions to the limit may seriously harm patients. Moreover, it is very doubtful that we shall find the limit in this manner.
A: Why not?
B: Well, a doctor diagnoses, then prescribes treatment, maybe major surgery, he carries out the treatment and he gets some results. Assume the result is a disfigured body that hobbles around for another five years and then dies. Who can tell the doctor that he has failed?
A: Studies with control groups.
B: And where will you get these control groups considering that physicians regard it as their duty to maim and patients regard it as their right to be maimed? Take the case of syphilis. For a long time it was thought to be a most dangerous illness. Before the arrival of modern antibiotics it was often treated in a way that severely damaged the organism. Yet it was found only quite recently that 85 per cent of the untreated

patients had a normal life span and that more than 70 per cent died without any evidence of the disease. The same may occur in other illnesses whose cure severely damages the organism. Many men have cancerous growth in their prostate glands. The growth remains confined to a small volume and does no harm. Doctors, especially in Germany, recommend regular biopsies – 'just to be on the safe side'. A biopsy often dislocates part of the growth, metastases arise in other parts of the body and more dangerous forms of cancer begin to spread. The same is true of many excisions of tumours and especially of the so-called Halstead method in the case of breast cancer. They are unnecessary, they set in motion dangerous and often uncontrollable processes. And all this because of assumptions the medical profession take for granted without even realizing the need for a closer examination.

A: So, what is the solution?

B: The solution is very simple – let people do what they want.

A: What do you mean?

B: There are many forms of medicine in this world.

A: You mean – witchdoctors and the like?

B: Well, things are not quite as simple as that. There are many forms of medicine which are not known to scientists but which proceed in an orderly way, are based on some kind of philosophy and have been around for quite some time.

A: Examples?

B: Examples are Hopi medicine, acupuncture, the various forms of herbalism that exist both in Europe and in the United States, faith-healing ...

A: Faith-healing? You cannot be serious.

B: What do you know about it?

A: Well, not much ...

B: And yet you cry bloody murder. Just listen. There are structural diseases, classified as circulatory ailments by Western medicine, that result in a displacement of the acupuncture meridians. The position of the meridians can be identified electrically – skin resistance is lower along a meridian. Now one has found that during the process of faith-healing the meridians of the healer become distorted in exactly the same way as in the patient – the faith-healer as it were takes over the illness, but his body is strong enough to overcome it and so in the end both he and the patient are cured. Then there is

homeopathy, there is water treatment and there are many more forms of medicine. They all have one thing in common: their methods of diagnosis do not interfere with the organism and their therapy is never as drastic as the therapy suggested by Western doctors. It is therefore advisable to try them first.
A: Do you seriously suggest that a physician send his patient to a witchdoctor . . .
B: Look, dear A, your terminology only shows how little you know about the history of medicine and the various medical schools in existence. You hardly know any medicine, you know little about science, but you think the right medicine is scientific medicine and damn the rest. You don't know anything about this rest either, but you say that it is no good, full of superstition, harmful and so you give it the worst possible name you can think of: you speak of 'witchdoctors', which, I am sorry to say, just reveals your ignorance. But the situation is much worse. So far I spoke only of what happens to people in Western societies – in England, in the USA, in France and so on. But the same ignorant aggressiveness tried to reform entire cultures and to adapt them to its ideas of a civilized life. Ever since people were discovered who did not belong to the circle of Western culture and civilization it was assumed, almost as a moral duty, that they had to be told the truth – which means, the leading ideology of their conquerors. First this was Christianity, then came the treasures of science and technology. Now the people whose lives were disrupted in this manner had already found a way of not merely surviving, but of giving meaning to their existence. And this way, by and large, was much more beneficial than the technological wonders which were imposed upon them and created so much suffering. 'Development' in the Western sense may have done some good here and there, for example in the restriction of infectious diseases – but the blind assumption that Western ideas and technology are intrinsically good and can therefore be imposed without any consultation of local conditions was a disaster. This, incidentally, is the reason why I always come up with astrology. I have no special love for astrology and much that is written in this area bores me to tears. But astrology is an excellent example of the way scientists deal with phenomena outside their area of competence. They don't study them, they simply curse them, insinuating that their curses

are based on strong and straightforward arguments. Now back to the case of medicine: patients in the West now very often must choose between alternative medical *opinions*. So why should they not extend their choice and choose between alternative medical *systems*? They will have to suffer the consequences, there is no assurance that scientific medicine has got the right answer, there is much reason to be afraid of the suggested treatment. Besides, alternative medical systems are often important parts of entire traditions, they are connected with religious beliefs and give meaning to the lives of those who belong to the tradition. A free society is a society in which all traditions should be given equal rights *no matter what other traditions think about them*. So respect for the opinions of others, choice of the lesser evil, chance of making progress – all these things argue in favour of letting all medical systems come out into the open and freely compete with science. And with this you have the answer to the question from which we started: who is going to determine what it means to be healthy and what it means to be sick? You said: physicians, scientific physicians. I would say that health and sickness are to be determined *by the tradition to which the healthy or sick person belongs* and within this tradition again by the particular ideal of life an individual has formed for himself. These particular forms of life can be studied scientifically only after they have been 'learned' and they must be learned as one learns a language, by participation in the activities that constitute it. Here the advantages of the old house physician who knew his patients, who knew their idiosyncrasies and their beliefs emerge very clearly: he knew what they needed and he has learned to provide it. Compared with him modern 'scientific' doctors are like fascist dictators who impose their own ideas of sickness and health under the cover of a therapy which in most cases is just an exercise in futility. So you see it is necessary, for all these reasons, to combine teaching, or the presentation of new views with protective devices. A good teacher will not just make people *accept* a form of life, he will also provide them with means of *seeing it in perspective* and perhaps of even *rejecting* it. He will try to *influence* and to *protect*. He will not only make propaganda for his views, he will add an ingredient that makes them less lethal and that protects people against being overwhelmed by them.

A: This is a most absurd theory – a psychological impossibility! You want to introduce new ideas. You speak in hostile surroundings. So you must make you case as strong as possible. And yet you want to add to the ammunition your opponents already possess ...

B: ... which of course must be defused as well! I admit that what I try to achieve may be Utopia. You see – I don't just want to replace maniacs of one kind by maniacs of a different kind – Jews by Christians, dogmatists by sceptics, scientists by Buddhists, I want to put an end to all manias and to the attitudes in people that support manias and make it easy for their prophets to succeed.

A: What attitudes do you have in mind?

B: I meet them constantly on my travels and at my lectures. I tell people that certain ways of arranging society are unwise and that the arguments for such arrangements are not valid ...

A: You just want to bamboozle them in your own way.

B: No. I analyse the views they hold, using arguments they understand and I show that the views do not work according to their own standards. And the question I always hear is: 'What shall we do now?'

A: A legitimate question.

B: For grown-up people?

A: Are you not speaking of students?

B: But this does not matter. If a person, eighteen years of age or older, when in a quandary asks 'What shall I do?', expects some lecturer to give him an answer and gets upset when the lecturer says 'Why don't you find out yourself?' then this shows to what extent our educational system is turning people into sheep, and intellectuals, teachers or what have you into sheepdogs.

A: But one day the sheep will grow up ...

B: ... and become sheepdogs barking at anybody who does not accept the faith they have received when still in the state of sheep – and this you call education?

A: How are people going to learn anything?

B: By informing themselves.

A: But then somebody must teach them ...

B: ... without turning them into flesh-and-bone copies of the manias of the teacher.

A: But there are many good and tolerant teachers, teachers who do not impose ideas, who are modest . . .
B: The modest ones are the worst.
A: Well, if you don't like modest teachers – what *do* you want?
B: You know that it was once thought that ideas had to be beaten into people's minds?
A: Yes. I have read about it – but these times have long gone by.
B: Now we have different methods.
A: We try to make the students interested, we try to adapt the teaching procedures to their natural development, their curiosities . . .
B: . . . and these modern teachers will of course be very modest.
A: They are. Critical and modest.
B: What do these modest teachers teach?
A: Well, physics, biology or what have you.
B: And in medicine?
A: Anatomy, physiology . . .
B: . . . acupuncture?
A: Certainly not.
B: Astrology?
A: We are speaking about science.
B: So, what your nice and modest teachers are doing is to bamboozle their students more efficiently. But the subject matter remains the same and is seen in the same one-sided manner. This applies not only to the teaching of science but to whatever is being taught, 'democratic virtues' included.
A: You mean you also object to the teaching of basic civic virtues?
B: Yes, I do – if the teaching is done in the manner described.
A: You object to the teaching of a humanitarian attitude?
B: If humanitarianism is not put in perspective, if people are not protected from it while being taught.
A: Well, how do you expect people to live together if they don't have certain basic commitments?
B: How do people succeed in not bumping into each other on the road?
A: Traffic laws.
B: Like driving on the right-hand side of the street.
A: Yes.

B: Are they committed to these laws?
A: Well, they have to obey them ...
B: What I meant was: do they think that driving on the right-hand side of roads is the only way to proceed, that it is an essentially human activity while driving on the left side is indecent, irrational, wicked, unjust?
A: Of course not – and now you want to say that ideas such as honesty, decency, truth should be viewed in the very same manner, as conventions necessary for preventing traffic accidents in society at large.
B: Not quite. I do not only want to explain their present function, I also want people to know something about their past performance, I want them to know about the things that were achieved with their help and about the things that were lost when the notions were introduced and enforced. One has to know their advantages as well as their disadvantages. I have no objection when individuals, or special groups choose to live on the basis of such notions entirely, when they choose to make truth their aim and damn the rest. That is their good right. But I object to turning local manias into foundations for society as a whole.
A: You object to humanitarianism?
B: I object to making humanitarianism part of the ideology of a society like the United States that contains people from many different traditions. And I object even more to the attempt to impose it on tribes and nations which live in a different way. By all means, let people hear about it, let preachers of humanitarianism try to convince them that it is the only creed worth considering ...
A: Well, what else is there?
B: Fear of God, for example, or harmony with nature, that is with all living things and not only with humans. A Western humanitarian is quite ready to maltreat animals so that he may find remedies to cure himself, while a person who respects the whole realm of nature denies the right of humans to subject other species to their whims even if this means a great disadvantage for them.
A: But if you don't teach people some virtues, how are they supposed to live together without killing each other?
B: I didn't say that virtues should not be taught, I said they should be taught like traffic regulations ...

A: This means you want people to act as if they were virtuous without being virtuous.
B: That is all that is needed for a society, even a world government, to work smoothly.
A: For example, you don't want to teach them respect for human lives, you just don't want them to kill people.
B: That might be an example.
A: You want society to consist of liars and play-actors.
B: If people wish to lie in domains not covered by the law, for example when they are not witnesses before a court of law, then that is their private business. Besides what I recommend does not automatically induce lying. If the law forbids killing – and that will be a traffic regulation as I said – then all that is needed is that the law be obeyed, *no matter what the reasons*. Some people may lie about their motives, others may openly say that they would like to kill everybody in sight but are not sure how to go about it, still others may confess that they have a grudge towards some people, would like to kill them but are even more averse to prison.
A: But how is this society going to work?
B: Crimes are punished and a strong police force guarantees that the laws are obeyed.
A: So, your apparent liberalism turns out to be restricted to ideas. In society at large suppression will be as bad as before.
B: Are traffic laws suppressive?
A: No, but . . .
B: And they have to be obeyed, and somebody has to take care of violators. *You* want to turn everybody into a zombie of virtue. Don't you realize that an education that achieves a state like that would be the most oppressive instrument in existence? It would obliterate all parts of a human being that do not agree with the virtue, it would turn him from a person capable of choosing between Good and Evil into a computer who always does the right thing. It would mean killing real people and replacing them by embodiments of ideas. No education known today has this effect, which is the reason why we have always needed a police. The education you are thinking of would replace external restrictions which control behaviour but leave minds unscathed by brainwashing procedures that put fetters on every part of a person. It is easy to see which procedure is more hostile to freedom.

A: And what laws, what commandments will be introduced into this society of yours?
B: This is not up to me to decide, it is up to the people who live in this society. And the suggestions will also change with the historical situation. Compromises will have to be made, a right balance will have to be found . . .
A: According to what criteria will you call this balance a 'right' balance?
B: Not *I* will call it a 'right' balance, the people concerned will call it a 'right' balance and they will call it a 'right' balance in accordance with criteria they may have to *invent* to deal with the situation in which they find themselves.
A: Your position is quite comfortable. First you talk big but when one asks you a more detailed question you reply it is not your business to make suggestions.
B: While your procedure – and now I mean you and your fellow intellectuals – is to develop theories, ethical systems, humanitarian philosophies and what have you in your offices and to impose them on others under the guise of an 'education', I want people to find their own way. All I do is to remove obstacles intellectuals have put in their path. You want to change behaviour until it agrees with your preconceptions. Naturally, you have to have a plan, while I can leave the structuring of society to its own institutions. By a proper education however I understand an instruction that tells people *what is going on* while at the same time trying to protect them from being overwhelmed by the tale. For example, it informs them that there is something like humanitarianism but it tries also to strengthen their ability to see the limits of this idea.
A: Can you give me an idea of the kind of instruction you have in mind? What are the protective devices you will use?
B: The devices change depending on the state of knowledge of the individual instructed. With small children you just start telling them fairytales: mythical, religious, scientific tales about the origin of the world and its structure . . .
A: So you already need a language and that language will have to be taught without your 'protective devices'.
B: Not at all! The best protective device against being taken in by one particular language is to be brought up bilingually or trilingually.

A: Very difficult!
B: Not at all difficult when the circumstances are right.
A: They hardly ever are right ...
B: They are often right, for example in certain parts of America and yet there is the overwhelming tendency to emphasize one language and to de-emphasize others. A child should grow up knowing not only various languages but also various myths, the myth of science included.
A: Which myths will you choose?
B: Again not *I* shall choose, but the people in the area and they will choose in accordance with their wishes.
A: But they need instruction how to choose.
B: Every group of people has its own wise men and its methods of choice – let them develop these methods.
A: Again you don't give an answer.
B: Because you again want me to impose a life on others ...
A: ... but this is what you are doing all the time.
B: No – all I say is: let people have their way and I criticize rationalists who want to push them in a different direction.
A: OK, proceed with your protective methods, so-called.
B: For grown-up people who have already certain beliefs humour is a great defusing force.
A: Is that why your books and articles are so full of bad jokes?
B: I am sorry my jokes don't please you but I did not write my articles for you. Humour is one of the greatest and most humane protective devices. Socrates understood this very well. In his *Apology* he develops his views but the moment they threaten to overwhelm the listener he defuses their effect with a joke. Aristophanes presented serious problems in comical form – he made people think but prevented them from falling for his views. Woody Allen in some of his more recent movies such as *Annie Hall* is a modern example. If the combination of humour and cognitive content is right then people are not at all put off by it – they understand the message, they take it seriously, they realize its limits. For Americans Mark Twain and Will Rogers are not just comedians, they are wise men. An example that shows very clearly the harm done by too intellectualistic an approach is Bert Brecht. He saw the role of humour, his theoretical writings contain most interesting and sensitive observations on it – but he failed. Another way of defusing a message is through a religion that reveals the great distance

between nature and the works of man. We are not only undercover agents in the society we inhabit and which never agrees completely with our being, we are also undercover agents in nature, always trying to adapt it to our simplistic conceptions and never succeeding. A religion that makes us aware of this situation is a powerful protective device against human conceit ...

A: What absurd ideas you come up with! Teaching by making people laugh about the things you teach, ruining science by confounding it with religion, man an 'undercover agent of the world and of society' ...

B: Well, quite obviously you never heard of such ideas.

A: And they are entirely unnecessary, for the protective devices you are looking for already exist and are much better than your fantastic notions.

B: So? And what might they be?

A: Critical rationalism.

B: Heaven help us!

A: Heaven help *you*! Critical rationalism gives you precisely the instruments you are looking for. It tells you that your attitude towards ideas should be a critical attitude; it tells you that theories will be the easier to criticize the more boldly they are presented. It encourages those who have new ideas to introduce them without precautions, in the strongest possible way. So you can have your cake and eat it too! You can make a strong case for your views, you don't need to hold back, you don't have to be careful and yet you don't need to be afraid that you will bamboozle your audience for the very strength of your presentation will make it easy for them to find faults – if they are critical that is.

B: It doesn't seem to work that way.

A: What do you mean?

B: Well, from your description one would assume that critical rationalists are free minds who write in a vigorous and lively style, who have considered the limits of rationality, who oppose science in its attempt to dominate society, who have found new ways of presenting their views, who make maximum use of media, film, theatre, dialogue in addition to the essay, who have discovered the function of emotions in discourse and many more such things. One would assume that they are part of a movement that is interesting, aids people in their desire for freedom and independence and brings out the best in them. Yet what I do see is just another dreary bunch of intellectuals writing in a constipated style, repeating *ad nauseam* a few basic phrases and being mainly concerned with the development of epicycles to such intellectualist monsters as verisimilitude and content increase. Their pupils are either frightened or nasty, depending on the kind of opposition they encounter, with a bare minimum of imagination. They do not *criticize,* that is, they do not invent ways of putting views in perspective; they *reject* what does not suit them with the help of standard speeches. If the topic is unfamiliar and cannot readily be dealt with they get confused like a dog who sees his master in unfamiliar clothing: they do not know – should they run, should they bark, should they bite him or should they lick his face. This philosophy is perfectly adapted to the mentality of young German intellectuals. These are very 'critical' people; they are against many things but they are much too afraid to bear responsibility for their attacks and so they look for some kind of security. Now what better security is there than the womb of an influential school that protects the critic from the repercussions of his criticism? And what better womb is there than critical rationalism, that even seems to have the authority of science on its side? True, it is not really a philosophy, it is confused rambling about science. True, the rambling is neither correct nor critical: there is not a single interesting event in the history of science that can be explained in the Popperian way and there is not a single attempt to see science in perspective. This 'philosophy' is nothing but a faithful but not very perceptive servant of science, just as earlier philosophies were faithful and not very perceptive servants of theology. Criticism is never directed at science as a whole (just as it was never directed at theology as a whole); most of the time it is directed either against rival philosophies or against unpopular developments in the sciences themselves – a conflict with the mainstream of science is avoided in either case.

All these drawbacks do not matter: our new intellectuals have neither the imagination nor the daring nor the historical knowledge to notice how badly *critical* rationalism fares when compared with the *tradition* of rationalism. Lessing was a rationalist, too – but what a difference! He was aware of the deadening influence of schools on thought and so he refused to become the founder of a school (in a similar way some early physicians who did not want their efficiency as healers to be impeded by adherence to the doctrines of a school regarded themselves as parts of a 'trend' that could go in any direction). Lessing realized the inhibiting influence of academic connections and so he refused to accept a professorship. He wanted to be 'free like a sparrow' even if that meant loneliness and starvation. Lessing noticed that a 'philosophy' that is a system of thought would only inhibit his inventiveness and so he let the case discussed determine the manner of discussion and not the other way around. Rationality for him was an instrument of liberation that had to be constantly rebuilt – it was not an abstract form to be imposed without regard to circumstances. Lessing admired some philosophies, such as Aristotle's account of the drama, but he was ready to modify them and even to drop them if a new entity in their domain, an as yet unheard combination of dramatic procedures, had enough inner life to suggest a change of standards. What a contrast between a free man like that and the anxious Popperian rodents that populate the German and the French intellectual scene! What a contrast in freedom, inventiveness, ability *and character*!

Lessing's philosophy was a *way of life*, his rationalism an instrument for improving thought as well as emotions, ideas as well as forms of expression, general principles as well as specific circumstances while Popperians restrict themselves to what they are pleased to call 'ideas' and even here are the slaves of a few ill-understood slogans about science. This is a school philosophy of the worst kind, a stupefying, enslaving, narrow-minded and uninformed ideology. Of course, school philosophies usually arise when ideas enter the academic scene – but in our case the originator of the school is not entirely without blame. Just consider the way in which Popper describes the origin in his ideas: there he was, a young thinker in Vienna, looking at the intellectual situation around him. He found Marxism, Freudianism and the theory of relativity. They were all impressive theories but he noticed a strange difference between them. He noticed that Marxism and Psychoanalysis seemed to be able to explain any fact in their domain. The theory of relativity, on the other hand, was constructed in such a manner that certain facts would mean its

demise. And here, young Karl realized, lay the difference between science and non-science: science is conjectural and falsifiable, non-science cannot be falsified. Am I right so far?
A: Yes – but I wish you would restrain your tendency to be sarcastic. These are important discoveries –
B: Whether they are discoveries and whether they are important we shall see in a minute. To start with, there was never a monster 'Psychoanalysis' as described by Popper. When Freud started out he was alone. He had certain ideas which he developed, tested, changed. The theory of Freud and Breuer is an early stage of this development. According to this theory hysteria is due to shocking events and can be cured by helping the patient to recall the events. The theory did not survive. It was discovered that recalling the event did not always suffice and it was also discovered that the alleged cures only replaced some symptoms by others. So, Freud changed his theory again. Then his pupils and collaborators started criticizing him. We got individual psychology and the psychology of Jung. The theory of relativity never led to such a proliferation of views and such a plethora of criticism. Quite the contrary, when the special theory of relativity ran into its first difficulty Einstein was unimpressed. He emphasized that the theory was simple, made sense to him, and that he was not going to give it up. Later on he ridiculed people who were impressed by 'verification of little effects' as he called test procedures in a somewhat mocking way. So, you see, Popper's account of the historical situation does not go very deep and is incorrect even at the surface . . .
A: But this is only the motivation . . .
B: Always distrust a person whose motives show that he does not know what he is talking about.
A: You have to do better than that! You have to show that the theory which Popper finally put forth was as inadequate as his motivation.
B: Which is not at all difficult! Popper claims he solved Hume's problem.
A: But he did solve it!
B: Maybe he did, maybe he didn't. At any rate, Erwin Schrödinger to whom Popper wanted to dedicate the English edition of the *Logic of Scientific Discovery* said he didn't.
A: How do you know?

B: I had lunch with Schrödinger. He had Popper's book with him; he pointed to it and exploded: 'Who does Popper think he is? He claims to have solved Hume's problem. He did no such thing. And now he wants to dedicate the book to me!'
A: Well, scientists are not the best judges of philosophical matters!
B: I agree – but when they support Popper the Popperians exclaim: 'Look how many Nobel Prize winners praise our beloved leader!' However, it does not matter if Popper solved Hume's problem. Solving Hume's problem has nothing to do with understanding the way in which science works.
A: Has nothing to do?
B: Has *absolutely* nothing to do. Hume's problem arises from a special philosophical position. Science started long before Hume, did not falter because Hume's problem was not solved and developed independently of the various suggestions made towards its solution. And we can easily understand why. Hume's problem is how a general statement can be justified on the basis of a finite number of its instances. And justification is supposed to be a procedure that obeys rules which can be spelled out in detail. Hume himself uses such rules when setting up his problem. But 'justification' in everyday life and in the more interesting parts of science does not have this feature. We do not 'establish' the character of a person by collecting instances of his behaviour and using rules to arrive at a general judgement, we as it were 'feel' our way towards it, and we have to, for the character of a person only rarely shows itself in an unambiguous way. For example, we may have reason to believe (and 'reason', here, does not mean instances) that he is a kind person, but on other occasions he seems to be heartless and cruel. We may disregard these occasions, assuming, without much evidence, that they are misleading and do not give us a true account of the man, we may explain them away by saying, again without much evidence, that his harshness was more than justified and thus not really cruelty.
A: All this belongs to the context of discovery – and everybody admits how this context is, and has to be, full of strange events ...
B: OK – but then you must also admit that what you call the context of justification – the situation when you have unambiguous and highly corroborated instances and a clear gen-

eralization and ask how the one is related to the other – is an ideal case that almost never occurs in practice, at least not in those parts of science which Popper loves – the realm of general abstract theory. What we have in practice is always a theory, which occasionally is formulated in very ambiguous terms (think of Bohr's older quantum theory!), evidence that points in all sorts of directions and a judgement which says what is reliable and what not and accepts the theory on that basis. The pure 'Humean' case almost never occurs and solving this case, therefore, does little to further our understanding of science. To use a more homely example, Hume's problem is how we justify 'All ravens are black' on the basis of n black ravens where n is some finite number. The problem which scientists face is what to do with 'All ravens are black' when what is given are n birds, most of them unambiguously ravens, some rather doubtful, though apparently ravens and of these ravens or pseudo-ravens some are grey, some black, some even white and some of a scintillating colour that can't be made out.

A: Well, the situation is clear – there are white ravens, hence, 'All ravens are black' is false.

B: That's how a philosopher would argue. Not so a scientist. 'All ravens are black' may fit into a theoretical system of great beauty and symmetry and so a scientist may retain it, despite the white ravens, and elaborate it further.

A: No scientist would do that!

B: Einstein did precisely that when his theory ran into trouble – and you have to be tough, otherwise you will never retain a single theory! So, you see, Hume's problem occurs in a dreamland that has hardly anything to do with the realities of science, just as Kant's moral imperatives construct a cruel dreamworld utterly different from our world in which honesty is restricted by kindness.

A: But what becomes of the philosophy of science if we assume such an attitude?

B: It withers away and is replaced by history and a philosophically sophisticated science that can take care of itself. Unfortunately the situation today is very different, though there are signs for hope here and there. What we have is a philosophically unsophisticated science that wants to take over the place religion and theology had before, a scientifically unsophisticated philosophy that praises it and is praised by the scientists in turn, a cowardly religion that has ceased to be a world view and has become a kind of social game and arts that shout 'Damn reality' and are only concerned with the sublime movements of the great artist's soul, even if its material effects are nothing more than Jackson Pollock urinations ...

A: Please, if we must argue, let's do it in an orderly way! You may be able to keep fifty ideas up in the air at the same time, but I can only deal first with one idea, then with another ...

B: And that is precisely what is the trouble with you and your friends the logicians! You can comprehend things only if they are presented in a certain order, preferably a linear order, the elements retaining their properties throughout the discussion. But what if the subject matter is shaped in an entirely different way? Take music. It is true that the various themes follow each other in a certain order but, first, their repetition very often is not an exact repetition, occasionally it takes considerable skill to recognize a theme through all its variations and, secondly, you have to pay attention to various things at the same time. Just look at the score of a symphony! Some people, for example the Dogon and some followers of C. G. Jung, think that the events of the world we inhabit are structured in exactly the same manner. Now if that is true, then people like you, who 'can only deal first with one idea, then with another' are at a serious disadvantage and they will have to learn thinking in a new way. Now you, at least, are honest, You admit to a certain deficiency, and you ask me to arrange our discussion in a manner that enables you to participate in it, despite your shortcomings ...

A: I didn't mean it quite that way ...

B: But you see my point, don't you? Now this request of yours, to adapt the discussion to your abilities, is of course perfectly legitimate. It is the most obvious request to make. Every rhetorician from Gorgias to Chairman Mao will tell a speaker that he must take his audience into account and present his ideas in a way most accessible to them. Your logicians, however, sing a very different song. They share your shortcomings, there are lots of things they don't understand and few things they do understand. But instead of trying to learn they assert that the things they do understand are the only things that can be understood. For some reason they have convinced almost everyone else that they are right and so we have now the strange spectacle of people without sight teaching everyone else the most efficient way of becoming as blind as they are. However, let us return to our main topic. What is our main topic?

A: You see, you wouldn't even be able to carry on a conversation with yourself unless somebody constantly helped you back to the starting point ...

B: No, no, wait a minute, I remember now. I said that science and scientific discoveries look important to us only because we have been conditioned to regard them as important, because they are ...

A: Stop right here, for now comes my first objection: I don't think it is conditioning to be impressed by the fact that man has been able to walk on the Moon....

B: How wrong you are! Can you imagine a prophet, or an early Christian, or even an average Dogon being much impressed by two men stumbling around on a dried out stone when he can talk to the Creator Himself? Or think of the Gnostics, the Hermeticists, or Rabbi Akiba who could direct their souls to leave their bodies and to rise from sphere to sphere to sphere, leaving the Moon far behind, until they faced God in all His Splendour. Why, these people would laugh their heads off at this strange enterprise where a tremendous amount of machinery, thousands of assistants, years of preparation are needed to achieve – what? A few clumsy and uncomfortable hops in a place no man in his right mind would want to see from close by ...

A: Come off it! Are you really going to compare the ravings of a few antediluvian maniacs with the scientific achievements of today?

B: How strange! First you pose as a rationalist who wants to argue and now that I give you some material for argument, you resort to abuse ...

A: Because you insist on making ridiculous statements. Or do you want me to believe that you take these theories seriously?

B: What I do and what I don't take seriously is not the issue here. The issue is whether we are impressed by the moonshots because we have been conditioned to be impressed by things of this kind, or because they are, how shall I say, 'intrinsically impressive'?

A: That is the issue.
B: Now, I gave you examples of people who because of their different background would have been anything but impressed by this celestial spectacle.
A: So?
B: Don't you see? If something is 'intrinsically impressive', then everybody must be impressed by it ...
A: Except when he is blinded by prejudice ...
B: And the early Christians were blinded by prejudice?
A: You can hardly call them objective.
B: Now 'being objective' for you means ...
A: Having an open mind.
B: Aha. Now tell me. Do you think you have an open mind?
A: Reasonably so, yes.
B: And having an open mind means being ready to examine the merits and demerits of views no matter now strange they may look at first sight, does it not?
A: Yes. But it does not mean confronting well established facts with weird fairytales and trying to get some argumentative mileage out of the confrontation. When I said the moonshots are impressive I did not mean they are impressive for any goon who happens to come along; I meant they are impressive for people with a certain minimum of education, people who have a rational basis for judging the problems and the achievements involved. Why, extending your argument one might as well deny significance to the moonshots because every dog on this earth went about his business as usual ...
B: And when you say that it is rational to regard the moonshots as impressive you assume that the astronauts really reached the Moon.
A: Of course.
B: While you doubt that anyone ever went past the Moon to God by spiritual projection.
A: Naturally.
B: And, of course, you have excellent reasons for assuming the one and doubting the other.
A: The best of reasons! Hundreds of people saw the rocket take off, millions saw the event on TV, tracking stations got in touch with the rocket the moment it was lost to unaided vision. Conversation was kept up with the astronauts . . .

B: And as regards your doubts concerning the reality of spiritual projection?
A: Why, you know as well as I do that such a thing is impossible.
B: *You* may know it, but *I* don't, so, please explain it to me.
A (*resigned*): I see you want to play games. OK, let's get it over with. As you told them, these stories assume that the soul leaves the Earth and rises from sphere to sphere to sphere until it encounters God? Do I repeat you correctly?
B: You do. The Book of Enoch assumes eight spheres, the tale of Rabbi Akiba three spheres, so there are various versions, but each of them assumes a series of spheres.
A (*triumphantly, though a bit puzzled by B's denseness*): There you are!
B: Yes?
A: There are no spheres!
B (*silent*).
A: Now have we at least settled that part of our conversation?
B: Have you heard of escape velocities?
A: Yes.
B: An escape velocity is the velocity needed for an object to escape the gravitational pull of another object and to leave it on a parabolic trajectory. Have you heard of Roche's boundary?
A: No.
B: Roche's boundary is the distance to which one planet can approach another planet without being torn apart, or tearing the other planet apart, whichever is bigger.
A: So?
B: So, here we have two kinds of 'spheres' around each celestial body, one in ordinary space, the other in momentum space, which might well represent the spheres in our stories.
A: But I very much doubt that the authors of the stories, whoever they are, had this interpretation of their spheres in mind.
B: Did Copernicus know the theory of relativity?
A: What are you up to now?
B: Well, tell me – did Copernicus know relativity?
A: You mean. Einstein's theory of relativity, or the more general idea of the relativity of motion?

B: Einstein's theory.

A: Well, the answer is obvious. Copernicus did not know Einstein's theory of relativity.

B: So, whatever he said cannot have been meant by him in an Einsteinian way.

A: No.

B: Tell me now – is Copernicus' theory correct?

A: Not entirely. He assumed a celestial sphere – that was a mistake. On the other hand he was quite right to say that the planets move around the Sun but that the Sun does not move around any one of the planets.

B: But according to the general theory of relativity there are no preferred reference systems. Hence the one description is as correct as the other and Copernicus is wrong.

A: That is a little too simple-minded. Of course, there is no absolute space. But a system in which the Sun is at rest is more nearly inertial than any system in which any one of the planets is at rest and in this respect different from the latter.

B: So, when saying that Copernicus 'was right to say that the planets move around the Sun but that the Sun does not move around any one of the planets' you give the words the interpretation you have just explained.

A: Yes.

B: And this interpretation, you say, was not the interpretation given to them by Copernicus.

A: It was not.

B: But you still use it in order to explain the achievements of Copernicus to a modern audience.

A: Not only that, I also need it if I want to derive Copernicus from Einstein as an approximation.

B: You realize, don't you, that what you are doing with Copernicus is precisely what I wanted to do with Enoch – but you objected.

A: And with good reason! For the tales of celestial navigation which you seem to be so fond of are not scientific theories ...

B: Before, or after the reinterpretation?

A: Before, *and* after the reinterpretation! It does not make sense trying to give factual content to a story when the story is in principle incapable of having factual content ...

B: Which assumes what we are examining: you are turning the proposition under debate into a premise of the argument ...

A: No, I am not, I am just adding a clarification and it is this: Copernicus is *intended to be* about actual events and it is therefore at least a *possible* factual statement, while your stories have an entirely different function, they have nothing to do with facts, they may not even be statements, they are religious fantasies, or allegories ...
B: You seem to know quite a lot about things you have never examined ...
A: I don't need to examine the matter in detail, I can work by analogy. For example, I know that a tragedy, such as the *Agamemnon*, is not the same as a historical account. A historical account is a series of statements which are supposed to tell what actually happened. A tragedy contains statements of an entirely different kind together with motions, background and so on and its purpose is ...
B: So now you are an expert on drama as well ... are you?
A: I am not, and I don't have to be, for all this is quite elementary ...
B: Which is precisely what the opponents of Galileo said when they criticized his theory of motion: 'All quite elementary, we all know that we would fall off the Earth if the Earth moved ...', and so on and so forth. You really are an excellent example of the attitude I was talking about above. Scientists have lots of 'arguments' in favour of the excellence of science but if one takes a closer look one realizes that many of their 'arguments' are nothing but dogmatic assertions about matters of which they have no knowledge whatsoever.
A: I wish you would stop moralizing and give me some real objections instead. OK. Let me try it in a different way: are there things such as myths and fairytales?
B: Of course there are.
A: Are such stories true, or are they not?
B: That is very difficult question ...
A: Oh, please, not this all-purpose scepticism again! Any conversation can be brought to a halt unless some things are taken for granted.
B: Agreed! And I am prepared to take a lot of granted – except the point at issue in our debate!
A: But this is just what I am talking about! We all know that there are some stories which report historical events, or events of nature, and other stories which are told for entertainment,

or as part of a ritual, and which have no factual content. Generations of thinkers have tried to make the difference between these two kinds of stories clear and now you act as if it did not exist!

B: I don't deny the distinction though I think it has done more harm than good. All I want to point out is that it is very difficult to decide whether a particular story such as the story of Enoch belongs to the one or to the other side of it. Most of the times the categories are thoroughly mixed up anyway. We may tell a story we believe to be historically true because we find it entertaining and instructive and yet we may discover later on that it never happened. Many cute stories from American history or, for that matter, from any other national history are of this kind. Or we may tell a story we are convinced never happened to make a moral point and then realize that the story is in fact true. For centuries stories from Homer's *Iliad* and *Odyssey* were used for inspiration, or to explain the qualities of true heroism, and nobody thought them to be more than delightful pieces of fiction until Schliemann found Troy by assuming certain parts of the *Iliad* to be literally true. Just recently it was discovered that some 'primitive' art works from sites in New Mexico, Arizona, Texas, California can be read as factual reports of the outburst of a nova that was also recorded in the Sun Dynasty in China. They can be read as factual reports – but this does not put them into the category 'factually true statements' – for the art works may well have had, *and most likely did have* a religious significance. Even modern scientific theories are not entirely 'pure', as one realizes when listening to a Nobel lecture, or inspecting the programme of the Pittsburgh Centre for the Philosophy of Science which displays Einstein's equations like a breviary displays the cross. So all these classifications are pretty superficial and practically useless. Take the case of the theatre which you mentioned. Detectives re-enact crimes to get at the truth. Piscator in Berlin did the same on a large scale and created a critical theatre that could be used for testing historical and sociological commonplaces. Brecht was interested in truth, but he was also interested in furthering the ability to discover error. He realized that some ways of presenting what claims to be the truth paralyse the mind while others further its critical abilities. A systematic account which harmonizes different aspects and uses standardized language belongs to the first category, a dialectical presentation which enlarges faults and lets different and incommensurable jargons run side by side belongs to the second.

So, there are different ways of making a statement, all of them have 'the same factual content', but they lead to very different attitudes towards this content. You may object. You may say that this happens in the theatre, but not in science: treatises such as Caratheodory on thermodynamics, or von Neumann on the quantum theory are attitude-neutral. Nothing could be further from the truth. To start with, von Neumann belongs to what one might call the Euclidian tradition which states basic assumptions and derives the rest from them. Arpad Szabó has shown that the Euclidian tradition originated with Parmenides. According to Parmenides things do not *change*, they *are*. A true presentation therefore cannot be a story that relates how things came into being, it cannot be a creation myth (such as the myth of Hesiod, or of Anaximander) and, in mathematics, it cannot be an account of the way in which mathematical entities are *constructed*. It must be an account that describes *unchangeable* natures and *unchangeable* relations between unchangeable natures. Now the basic postulate of this tradition – things do not change – has been dropped long ago. We have realized that there are no stable forms, no unchangeable laws of nature and we now assume that even the universe as a whole has a history. The basis of the Euclidian tradition is no longer acceptable. Has this influenced our attitude towards mathematics and mathematical physics? It has not. Von Neumann's presentation, which has many followers, still reflects the older ideologies. Moreover, it reflects them in a way that makes it very difficult to discover basic faults and to imagine alternatives. One becomes convinced, as was Parmenides, that there must be one perfect way of saying things, and that one has almost reached it: one more step, or two more steps *in the same direction*, and the truth will reveal itself.

But now take an essay by Bohr. To start with, Bohr's essays, even though dealing with highly technical matters, are written in an informal and unfinished style. Von Neumann, of course, is also unfinished, and occasionally this is even admitted, but there are parts which seem to be definitely settled, and not in need of any further examination. These parts are conspicuous by the conciseness and the clarity of their formulation. No such special formulations exist in Bohr – everything is equally open to doubt. Philosophy and science are mixed up in a manner that has displeased such purists as Thomson and Rutherford. There is a series of suggestions, each of them throwing light on a different aspect of the problem treated, none of them claiming finality. All this is quite intentional. Bohr knew that our thinking is always unfinished, and he wanted to make this obvious, not hide it. He also knew that every solution, every so-called 'result' is only a transitory stage in our quest for knowledge. It was created by this quest, it will eventually be dissolved by it. It is for this reason that his essays are *historical* essays – they report a series of discoveries and errors and slowly move towards the present state of things; they do not move towards anything like a 'final solution'. The description of past achievements and present 'results' is just as tentative and unfinished as the description of the stages that led up to them.

Now compare Bohr and von Neumann. Is it not almost like two different novels written about events which are only loosely related to each other? And yet both works are contributions to one and the same subject – quantum mechanics. Moreover, they influence this subject not merely by the *facts* they contain, but also by their *style*. It was the *style* of Bohr and of his followers which gave the older quantum theory its particular flavour and which was responsible for the innumerable discoveries, retractations, daring hypotheses and profound observations that characterize this fascinating period of research. The followers of von Neumann proved lots of interesting theorems with little application to concrete cases, while the followers of Bohr have always stayed very close to physical reality though in doing so they were forced to use terms in an intuitive and imprecise way. All this means that the aesthetic or 'dramatic' elements which separate Bohr from von Neumann are not external embroideries which should perhaps be phased out, they are essential for the development of science itself.

Distinctions of the kind you mention, if they can be drawn at all, must therefore be drawn in a way very different from the customary way, and with a very different purpose in mind.

Take tragedy, which seems to be on the opposite side of the spectrum. It seems to be – but it is not. For the Greeks the *Persians* was a dramatic reminder of very important *historical* events, but the form was not the only one in which historical events were presented. Aristophanes talks about the politics of his time, even about living contemporaries, but in a style that is very different from the style of Aeschylus. You know that Plato objected to poetry and that he wanted it removed from his ideal state. His reasons were that poetry leads away from true reality, arouses emotions, and beclouds thought. But he granted that there might exist some argument for retaining it, and he challenged 'her champions' – these are his words – 'who love poetry, but are not poets, to plead for her in prose'. Aristotle took up the challenge. Tragedy, he said, is more philosophical than history; it does not only report *what* happened, it also explains *why* it had to happen and thus reveals the structure of social institutions. This perfectly describes the *Oresteia* of Aeschylus. The trilogy shows that institutions may paralyse action. Orestes must avenge his father – he cannot avoid this obligation. To avenge his father he has to kill his mother. But to kill his mother is as fearful a crime as the crime he is called upon to avenge. Thought and action are paralysed – unless we change the conditions which dictate what must and what must not be done – and such a change is indeed suggested towards the end of the trilogy. Note the form of the 'argument': there is a set of possible actions. Each action leads to an impossibility. So our attention is directed towards the principle that demands the actions and yet declares them to be impossible. The principle is revealed, an alternative is suggested. Arguments of this form are found in Xenophanes and later on, in a more explicit form, in Zeno (paradoxes of motion). They underlie some modern set-theoretical paradoxes, such as Russell's paradox.

Thus we may say that the trilogy combines a factual account of social conditions with a criticism of these conditions and the suggestion of an alternative. According to Aristotle it does even more. Plato had objected to poetry because of the emotions it arouses. Aristotle points out that the emotions have a positive function: they release tensions that interfere with clear thought (katharsis) and aid the mind in remembering the structures revealed by the play, they aid it in remembering its philosophical (i.e. its factual-theoretical) content. All this is done with the help of a story, which for the Greeks was an important part of their tradition, and perhaps even of their history. Now, my dear friend, how are you going to classify such a complex entity? Its outer appearance makes it a work of art (or of acted-out history), at least according to the manner in which we classify things today. Its *structure* (individual names now being taken as variables, as has been suggested by Lévi-Strauss) makes it a factual statement combined with a criticism applied in accordance with a rather sophisticated logic. There is dramatic impact, re-enactment of tradition, factual content, logic – and I now mean *formal* logic and not the inane 'logic of aesthetic discourse' which some ignoramuses want to lay on us – all united into a powerful and most sophisticated entity. The traditional accounts give superficial descriptions of a tiny aspect of the whole and neglect the rest. This is why works of art as described by the aesthetician or by the philosopher of the arts look so vapid when compared with the real article.

Now you might object that whatever factual content is involved is not *stated*, but rather *hinted at* in a roundabout way. But in science such an indirect 'hinting at' is not at all unusual: take Bohr's atomic model of 1913. Does it assert or 'state' that the hydrogen atom consists of a nucleus in the centre of a circular trajectory that may abruptly change its diameter? It does not, for Bohr knew very well that such a statement would be false, for theoretical as well as for experimental reasons. Still, the model is not without factual content. How is this factual content obtained? Via a complex method of interpretation which is largely guesswork (and was therefore never spelled out in detail) and which later on became known as the 'principle of correspondence'. Exactly the same is true of the liquid drop model of the atomic nucleus. There is even the element of falsifiability and of falsification you Popperians make such a fuss about. After all, the trilogy reveals certain difficulties and removes them by a new 'hypothesis', by a new way of living together. The premises are not neatly written out as they are in the textbooks' examples of falsification; they have to be found. But if anything, this makes the *Oresteia* more comprehensive than the textbooks. It tells us how the premises can be found *and* how they are to be evaluated, and not only the former. Mind you, I do not admit for a moment that falsificationism is better than a method that guarantees stability – but it is interesting to see that it may turn up in the middle of a 'work of art' where nobody would have expected it.

Now considering this complex character of myths, tragedies, of the Homeric epics, one asks oneself why it was ever attempted to create an abstract entity, 'knowledge', and to separate poetry from it. This is a most interesting question to which one fine day I hope to find the answer. The general outline of the answer is simple. We know there was a period in Greece when the philosophers tried to replace the poets as intellectual and political leaders. Plato refers to this period when talking of the 'long-lasting quarrel between philosophy and poetry'. Philosophers were a new class, with a new ideology which was fairly abstract, and they wanted to make this ideology the basis of education. They did not use arguments, but they used a myth to discredit the opposition. They myth asserted (a) that poetry was impious and (b) that it had no content: the 'wise men' of earlier ages simply had not said anything. This is of course a simplification, but I think it catches some features of the transition.

Now the problem is: why were the philosophers so successful? What was it that gave them the upper hand so that poetry in the end seemed to be mere emotionalism, or symbolism, without any content whatsoever? It cannot have been their power of argument, for poetry, *interpreted properly*, contained arguments its own.

Similiar observations can be made about the rise of seventeenth-century science. In this case the moving force was the rise of new classes who had been excluded from the pursuit of knowledge and who turned the exclusion to their advantage by asserting that it was *they* who possessed knowledge, not their opposition. Again this idea was accepted by everyone, in the arts, in the sciences, in religion, so that we have now a religion without ontology, an art without content and a science without sense. But I digress. What I wanted to emphasize is that the classifications on which you rely, while perhaps adequate for describing the desiccated *modern products* of these ancient power struggles (modern fairytales, such as the fairytales of Oscar Wilde; modern myths, such as twentieth-century Marxism or modern astrology; modern science, such as sociology) do not give a correct account of the *ancient opponents* of this power struggle (ancient myths, fairytales, etc.) and of those features of modernity which have still retained some trace of the complexity of the ancient material (science as practised by Bohr, Lévi-Strauss, C. G. Jung). Moral: one should not deny factual content to a point of view because it seems to fall into the myth–fiction–religion–fairytale-basket of the distinction. Examine each case on its own merits, and there will be surprises without end ... But you have become rather silent and thoughtful. It can't be that I have convinced you at last!

A: You have convinced me that the specific arguments I used to show that Enoch and similar stories cannot be factual were faulty, but I don't think that my suspicions were unfounded. As a matter of fact, I think I have now a much better argument than I had before. You see, *before* I was ready to concede that the inventors of these stories were rather imaginative, that they were great poets, but that they were rational people, not madmen. Now, taking their stories literally and giving them empirical content, I am forced to conclude that they must have been out of their minds. For what do these stories tell us? They talk about the actions of gods, demons and of other weird and unwieldy creatures, they seem to be unaware of the simplest causal laws while constructing fantastic connections such as a connection between rain-dancing and the weather, they involve oracles and the assumption that the people themselves used these oracles in their daily affairs, and so on. Stories of this kind occur even among the Greeks who certainly were one of the most rational people that ever lived, who had eyes to see and a mind to figure out what they had seen. I prefer to assume that their world view corresponded to their capacity, and so I prefer to interpret their *myths* as *poetry*. You, who seem to believe in the rational unity of mankind and who have more than once objected to the idea that people became intelligent only in Hellenistic times, when the sciences were rather advanced, should see the force of this argument.

B: That is a strange way of arguing indeed. But now I have ceased to expect a rationalist to behave in a rational manner.

A: What do you mean?
B: You don't see? Well, let me spell out the details. You want to convince me that certain stories such as the story of Enoch cannot possibly have factual content. So – what do you do? Do you analyse them in greater detail? No. Do you present an argument? No. You tell the story in a sneering way *insinuating* that only a madman could assume them to be true. I am not surprised when I find such procedures at the London School of Economics, where after three generations of critical rationalism basic argument has deteriorated into a few standard rituals. But you, I thought, were a somewhat more reasonable person, and not quite so firmly tied to the prayers of The Faithful. Do I really have to tell you that what you are offering is not an argument, and do I have to remind you that this was precisely the way in which Galileo's less gifted opponents treated his astronomy?
A: The case of Galileo is quite irrelevant here. Galileo *founded* science and so, naturally, he was in a more precarious position than we are today. We, on the other hand, have a bulk of sound scientific knowledge at our disposal and we can criticize views by comparing them with this bulk. This is what I had in mind, though I may have been too fast for you to notice. And having made this simple criticism, why should I not make fun of an opponent who is too dense to see the point?
B: Perhaps 'the point', as you call it, is not as simple as you think. You say we can criticize myths by comparing them with a 'bulk of sound scientific knowledge'. I take this to mean that for every myth you want to criticize there exists a highly confirmed scientific theory, or a set of highly confirmed scientific theories that contradicts the myth and belongs to the 'bulk'. Now if you look at the matter a little more closely you will have to admit that *specific* theories incompatible with an interesting myth are extremely hard to find. Where is the theory that is incompatible with the idea that rain-dances bring rain? Of course, this idea runs counter to some basic *beliefs* of the great majority of scientists, but as far as I can see these beliefs have not yet found expression in *specific theories* that could be used to exclude them. All we get is a vague though very strong *feeling* that in the world of science rain-dances cannot possibly work. Nor is there any set of *observations* that contradicts the idea. And, mind you, watching rain-

dances fail *today* is not enough. A rain-dance must be carried out with the proper preparation and in the proper circumstances and these circumstances include the old tribal organizations and the mental attitudes corresponding to them. The Hopi theory makes it very clear that with the break-up of these organizations man lost power over nature. Thus rejecting the idea of the efficiency of rain-dancing simply because rain-dancing does not work under present conditions is like rejecting the law of inertia because no object is seen to move on a straight line with constand speed.

Here the opponents of Galileo were in a much, much better position. They had theories, well formulated theories and not just vague feelings as to what is 'scientific' and what is not, and they had facts. Facts and theories taken together formed a 'bulk of sound scientific knowledge' of the kind admired by you and this bulk was inconsistent with Galileo's views. Their objections to Galileo were much stronger than your objections *vis-à-vis* the myths that have come down to us. *And yet they were defeated*.

Thus you not only *lack* the material for a proper criticism of rain-dancing, you also have wrong ideas about the way in which such material *should be used*. Moreover, the best of Galileo's opponents knew his views very well, they were expert astronomers. Which of you rationalists has ever studied the views you condemn so blithely with equal care? Now I know, of course, that merely chiding you will not do, so let me give you some examples of what you might find when taking a closer look at the areas you now reject out of hand. Take the idea that comets portend wars. An utterly ridiculous idea – isn't it? No rhyme and reason to it. Prejudice pure and simple. But let us look at the matter a little more closely! Comets were regarded as atmospheric phenomena, as a kind of fire in the upper layers of the atmosphere. Now if this assumption is true then a comet will draw material towards the upper regions and there will be large-scale atmospheric movements, starting at the ground, and reaching all the way up. Such movements may give rise to storms and they may also manifest themselves in a colouring of the atmosphere at dusk, or at dawn, depending which side of the Sun the comet is on. Remember the other day, when there seemed to be fire all over Mount Tamalpais and when the colours of leaves assumed a dark and saturated hue. This is the phenomenon I am talking about. Moreover, the motions of the atmosphere and the excessive fire in it will disturb its normal composition and affect the metabolism of man and beast. Animals are particularly sensitive, and they notice the change long before the comet becomes visible, just as they notice an earthquake in advance. There will also be a greater propensity for plagues, the heating of the air will lead to a corresponding heating of minds, it will lead to an increase of irresponsible decisions by men in power which means: war. Now it is quite possible that four or five different comets were accompanied by the phenomena described. As a matter of fact Kepler, who had amassed a large amount of relevant material, noticed such correlations and used them in his attempt to build up an empirical astrology. Thus the basic assumption about comets is confirmed. But this assumption is also theoretically plausible, for it agrees with the theory of elements which in turn gives a good qualitative account of macroscopic phenomena. This being the case one will not object if one finds some refuting instances – after all, even in our science refuting instances are often shelved pending further examination. As a result we have a hypothesis, a connection between comets and wars which at first sight seems outlandish and silly but which on further investigation reveals theoretical ingredients and evidence that make it rational, given the material available at the time, though not acceptable to us who possess different and, so we believe, better material. Let us call a hypothesis of this kind a hypothesis of type *A*. Now take the idea that the world is full of gods, that the gods interfere with physical phenomena and occasionally reveal themselves to man. Another fantasy, another dream, you will say. Let us see! – Have you ever been angry?

A: Many times! Especially ...

B: Don't tell me. Now: how did you experience your anger?

A: What do you mean?

B: Well, did you experience it as something produced by yourself, or as something that entered you from the outside, and when I say 'from the outside' I don't mean: passing through your skin. What I mean is: did it feel as if it arose from inside yourself, or as if it were something alien happening to you?

A: I really don't know – which is strange, for I have been very angry, and quite recently ...

B: There goes another beautiful theory!
A: What theory?
B: The theory that anger is a mental event and that we are directly acquainted with all features of a mental event. Now, do you know a phenomenon called the 'subjective eye grey'?
A: No.
B: You go into a dark room. You adapt to the darkness. When you are finally dark-adapted, your field of vision will not be absolutely dark, it will be greyish, in the form of a cylinder, with your body as the main axis.
A: Ah, I remember now – I once participated in an experiment of dark-adaptation and the guy asked me to describe what I saw after I had been left in the room for half an hour.
B: And what did you see?
A: A few bright spots here and there, but not a trace of your cylinder. I was told that was to be expected and I was trained to see the phenomenon. The training was quite interesting. The experimenter put a heated wire in the field of vision, but he did not heat it sufficiently to make it appear red. It appeared a greenish grey – the radiation was too weak to stimulate the colour receptors, he said. Then he told me to pay attention to the neighbourhood of the wire, to its right and to its left. I noticed that the glow did not end where the wire ended, but spread beyond it, receding into the background as the distance from the wire increased. And then the current was turned down until the wire could no longer be seen. Yet the glow remained, and I can now see it every time, after dark-adaptation. It even looks like a physical surface, like the sky on a clear summer evening. Moreover, I have the curious feeling that the phenomenon was there all the time, but that I was too dense to notice it. Like after-images which intermingle with our vision at all times but which must be brought to our attention by special methods.
B: An excellent description of a truly marvellous series of events! You start out with some indistinct impressions, you are instructed, and you end up with a phenomenon which almost seems to be the perception of a physical object.
A: Yes, and that reminds me of another occasion when something similar occurred. Long ago I wanted to become a biologist; my father bought me a rather expensive microscope and

when I looked into it I thought that I had been cheated. The pictures in the biology books had been so clear, but I saw nothing that even faintly resembled them. There was a chaos of lines and motions and I was not even sure whether the motions occurred in my eyes which I strained to see what I wanted to see, or whether they were *objective motions* ...
B: Do you know that this was exactly the way in which the first observers who looked at the sky through the telescope described what they saw?
A: I did not know that. Galileo does not speak in this manner, at least I don't remember ...
B: He does not, for not everyone experiences the same phenomena under the same circumstances. What he saw was quite definite, but no less illusory – just look at his drawing of the moon, here in the *Sidereus Nuncius*.
A: Amazing – what is this gaping hole doing in the middle of the Moon?
B: This is what Galileo saw, described, and drew. You will not be surprised to hear that other observers saw something entirely different, and that he was not able to immediately convince his opponents of the reality of the 'Medicean Planets', as he called the moons of Jupiter. He instructed them how to look through the telescope, he told them what was to be expected, but only some people saw what he said he had seen, and they were not convinced of the reality of the phenomena either. Aristotle had foreseen all these problems and the strange and ambiguous nature of the first telescopic observations would not have surprised him at all. According to Aristotle the forms of an object travel through a medium to the sense of the observer. A first condition for a clear and veridical perception is that there be no disturbances in the medium. Furthermore, one perceives things properly only under certain 'normal' circumstances in which the senses are adapted to the objects. Neither condition is satisfied in the case of telescopic vision. Aristotelians were therefore as justified in refusing to look through a telescope and in taking seriously what they saw as a modern physicist would be when refusing to accept the result of an experiment carried out with unknown equipment. These facts are hardly ever mentioned in the historical accounts. The psychology of perception is hardly ever utilized

by historians of science and philosophy. But now, please, continue with your story which illustrates some important principles of this subject.

A: Well, when I did not see what I had expected to see, I complained to my biology teacher. He calmed me down saying that this difficulty was experienced by everyone and that I had to *learn to see*. He first gave me some very simple things to look at, a hair, a grain of sand, and he instructed me to use the lowest magnification. I had no problems. He told me to increase the magnification and to stay with the same objects. I shrunk back when I saw my own hair like a cosmic rope stretching across an enormous sky – but I saw it alright. And so we gradually went on to more and more complicated objects and today I not only recognize the most intricate organisms, as if they were old friends I had left only a few hours ago, I am even incapable of seeing the confusion with which I started. Everything I see under the microscope is now firmly objective.

B: Now let us return to your experience of anger. You have described two processes of learning to see. In both cases you started with an indistinct impression that was clearly subjective and ended up with well structured objective phenomena. And I now use the words 'subjective' and 'objective' to describe how things *looked* to you, not how they actually *were*. The subjective eye grey, you said, 'even looked like a physical surface, like the sky on a clear summer evening' although we both agree that there is no such surface. Do you think that your feelings of anger could be changed in a similar way?

A: I am sure of it. After all, we say that somebody was 'overcome by anger' or 'shaken by grief' which indicates that the experience of anger and grief must at some time have been much more decidedly 'objective' than it seems to be today.

B: Would it surprise you if I told you that the Greeks experienced anger and remembered dreams as objective events that occurred to them, sometimes against their will?

A: It would not surprise me at all.

B: Now, let us go one step further. When you first looked into the microscope, did you have an idea of what you might see?

A: Most certainly. I had read biology books with beautiful pictures of all sorts of ghastly creatures in them.

B: And though these pictures were very clear, you saw nothing

that even faintly resembled them when you looked into the microscope.
A: Yes, that was my big disappointment.
B: But you were instructed, and your impressions changed, until they became stable and objective.
A: Yes.
B: And if you had been brought up with microscopes tied to your eyes, your impressions would have been stable from the very beginning, at least as far as you can remember.
A: Agreed.
B: Now, then, let us look at the gods of Homer. Are there descriptions, or pictures of them?
A: Yes, there are – the *Iliad* and *Odyssey* are full of descriptions, and there are pictures and statues all over our museums.
B: And the descriptions and pictures are clear, and definite?
A: They are strange – but they are certainly most clear and definite.
B: And yet we don't experience anything that even faintly resembles them.
A: And there is a good reason for it: the gods don't exist!
B: Not so fast, not so fast, my friend! Remember, we are now talking about *phenomena, not* about 'reality'. And remember also your own description of the subjective eye grey: it 'looked like a physical surface' despite the fact that people in dark rooms are not surrounded by surfaces of this kind. So, I repeat: we have clear and distinct descriptions of the gods, but there is nothing in our experience that even faintly resembles the objects of these descriptions.
A: I guess I shall have to agree with you.
B: Now in the case of the microscopic images and in the case of the subjective eye grey there exists an instruction that creates phenomena of precisely the kind reported by the descriptions. We can *learn* to see the world in accordance with the descriptions.
A: And now you want to convince me that there is an instruction that may enable us to experience divine phenomena.
B: Precisely – but again, the situation is not at all simple. Remember the caveat I raised in the case of the rain-dances: the ceremonies work only if the proper circumstances are first realized. There must be tribal associations of the right kind, accompanied by the right attitudes. The same applies to our

present case. It may be very difficult, and perhaps impossible, to make *you* see gods, or to experience their power. The Greek gods were tribal gods, and they were nature gods. Social circumstances, your upbringing, the general spirit of the age make it almost impossible to understand, let alone to bring to life their first aspect – and where is the 'nature' that would aid you when trying to realize their second?

A: Is this not a decisive objection against their existence?

B: Not at all. To see the right things you need the right instruments. To see distant galaxies you need telescopes. To see gods you need men, properly prepared. Galaxies don't disappear when telescopes disappear. Gods don't disappear when men lose their ability to get in touch with them. To say 'God is dead' or 'The great Pan is dead' because they are no longer experienced would be just as silly as saying that neutrinos don't exist because we no longer have the money to repeat Reynes's experiment.

A: In the case of the neutrino we have convincing *indirect* evidence ...

B: Because we have theories, highly complex theories about them! As usual you start the argument from the wrong end. You say: there is neither direct nor indirect evidence for the gods, so we should not theorize about them. But it is clear that indirect evidence is indirect evidence *for a theory*, so there must be a theory in the first place, and the theory must be rather complex, otherwise we would hardly talk of *indirect* evidence. This means we must start building complex theories before the question of indirect evidence is ever raised. Direct evidence, however, depends on instruments, or on well prepared observers – and how shall we build the instruments, or prepare the observers, if there is no theory to guide us? But to return to the question how one can be made to experience the gods. As I told you it may be impossible to make you *see* gods, or to *experience* their influence, but it may perhaps be possible to make you *understand* how people who live in the right circumstances may have strong experiences of the presence of gods. Let me start with what you said about your own anger. You said that you are often angry, even very angry, but that you do not know whether the anger you experienced was something 'objective' that forced itself upon you against your own will, or whether it was part of yourself.

A: I think I must correct my description, for now that the question has been posed the phenomena seem to be a little more definite.
B: What do you mean by that? Has your *anger* changed: or has the *memory* of your anger changed?
A: It is almost as if my anger, in retrospect, were one of those ambiguous pictures which you can see now in one way, now in another. Something changed – and one does not quite know what. And this, I think, applies to all experiences. You know there was a time when despite all attempts to approach my private affairs in a rational manner I was completely dominated by emotions, by very strange emotions ...
B: Don't tell me you made a fool of yourself over a woman!
A: Not one, but many. And not for a year, or for two years, but for almost fifteen years ...
B: What do you know! A critical rationalist being led by the nose by emotions! Well, I always said: reason is the slave of the passions ...
A: But it isn't – that is what I want to tell you! You see, what amazed me about this feeling people call 'love' was its lack of articulation. It was a strong force that directed my actions, but any attempt to get some insight into the *quality* of this force, to discover its 'face' as it were made it change its character in the most surprising way without leaving me with anything definite to comprehend, or to come to terms with. Finally I got quite annoyed ...
B: I bet you did!
A: ... and I asked myself whether there was a way of as it were catching the phenomenon, of giving it shape, of making it stable and comprehensible. I thought of psychoanalysis for I had heard that it changes not merely one's attitude towards mental phenomena, but the mental phenomena themselves, but all the psychoanalysts I met were such idiots, so I gave up the idea. Then by accident I came across a story by Heine where he describes a feeling that starts as a strong attraction, turns into loathing without losing its attracting propensities, and I realized that this was precisely what I had experienced in one particular case. Reading the description had changed my experience without really changing it and I *understood* what had happened during this particular affair. I read other poets: Byron, whom Heine had admired, Grillparzer, Jean

Paul, Oscar Wilde, Ezra Pound, Marinetti, even Goethe, and I found them to be veritable handbooks of phenomenological descriptions of strange processes *which became real only by virtue of these descriptions*. I think I now agree with Börne who said that history would be nothing without the historian who *writes down* what has happened and so *shapes the events, defines them*, even for the participants.

B: This is precisely the situation I have in mind. Most of our thoughts, feelings, perceptions are ill-defined to a surprising extent. We do not notice this lack of definiteness just as we do not notice the blind spot of our eyes: everything seems perfectly clear. But let somebody ask an unusual question, or give an unusual account of his experiences, and we realize that this apparent clarity is just a reflection of ignorance and superficiality. Yet the amorphous material that is our consciousness is capable of improvement, it can be put into a more definite shape by questions, descriptions, systematic accounts, education. Just as the sculptor starts with the shapeless marble stone, works on it until he finally presents us with a delicate and complicated statue, in the very same way the educator starts with the shapeless state of mind of his pupils and impresses upon it ideas and phenomena he regards as important. We go through a wood; suddenly the wood opens, we find ourselves on the top of a mountain, surveying a vast landscape. We experience a feeling of awe. This feeling is not too well defined, it is like a passing mood. Now assume we have been brought up to believe in a god who not only created the universe, but who is present in it, to protect it, to insure its continued existence. We see no longer an arrangement of material objects, we see part of divine creation and our feeling of awe becomes an objective perception of divine elements in nature. Or assume you walk through a wood during the night, far away from highways and city lights. You see dark shadows, hear strange sounds, you have a feeling of being close to nature, nature 'speaks to you'. Usually this feeling is subjective and sentimental, one has read poems which 'make her speak' and the vague memories of the poems mingle with the even more vague impressions of the present, giving rise to an indistinct and inarticulate state of mind. Assume on the other hand, you have been brought up in the belief that the wood is full of spirits, you have walked through it quite often when you were young, your parents explained to you the nature of the sounds, the nature of the spirits that produce them and told you the traditional stories. That gives substance to the impressions, turns them into more definite phenomena, just as the biological instruction gives substance to the vague microscopic images. Now turn inward. There are thoughts, feelings, fears, hopes, memories, all of them vague and homeless in the sense that we do not know *or even care* whether they come from us or from some other agency – they seem to belong neither to the subject, nor to an objective world. But assume you have been taught that the gods may speak to you while you are awake, or in dreams, that they may give you strength when you least expect it, that they make you angry so that you carry out their plans with greater vigour, assume you have been trained to listen to their voices, to expect definite answers and that you have been given examples of such answers – assume all this, and your internal life will again become more definite, it will cease to be a hardly noticed interplay of cloudlike shapes and become a battlefield of the clear and distinct actions of the gods. Looking at Greek literature we see that this was indeed the way in which the Greeks experienced their surroundings, and their 'inner life'. Their experience of the material universe was the experience of a world full of gods. Gods were not just fanciful ideas, they were parts of the phenomenal world. The experience of self, too, was an experience of divine forces and messages and this to such an extent that the notion of an autonomous self, even of a single, coherent *body* was unknown to the Greeks at the time of Homer.

So far I have been talking about *phenomena* only. Now the phenomena I have described lend strong support to the *hypothesis* that 'Everything is full of gods' as Thales is said to have expressed himself. The hypothesis differs from the hypothesis on comets I mentioned earlier, and so I shall call it a hypothesis of type *B*. The hypothesis about comets can be changed by research, for example by a measurement of distance, leaving phenomena and fundamental concepts unchanged. But research alone cannot change the divine hypothesis. To effect such a change we must introduce new fundamental *concepts* which clash with the Homeric world experience, and we must also start *seeing* things in a different way. We must replace the colourful universe of Homer by the barren industrial fumes of Anaximander, we must replace his lively gods by the totalitarian monster of Xenophanes and Parmenides, so much beloved by our critical rationalists, we must arrange our impressions in different ways also which means that ancient phenomena, the world of gods, spirits, heroes *will have to be dissolved*. And, mark you, we do not just remove the gods from a material world that can exist without them and whose behaviour remains unchanged, we also introduce a *new kind of matter* that is barren and inert and no longer the seat of life-giving forces. *A whole world disappears* and is replaced by phenomena of an entirely different kind.

There is still a further type of hypothesis to be considered, and it is perhaps the most interesting one. Hypotheses of this type – I shall call them type *C* – are hypotheses which though embedded in a mythical tradition and though in conflict with science *turn out to be correct when translated into scientific language*. Such hypotheses were discovered quite recently when acupuncture turned out to be a successful method of treatment for ailments which Western medicine could not even diagnose. This led to further research and to the discovery of a great variety of medical 'schools', each of them containing knowledge not available to science. The knowledge may be practical only, but it may also contain a sizeable theoretical component. Such theories are very interesting, they show that science is not the only way of acquiring knowledge, that there are alternatives, and that the alternatives may succeed where science has failed. Then there is the whole field of parapsychological phenomena. There are two reasons why this field is of interest for our present debate. On the one hand, many phenomena described by, or presupposed in myths are parapsychological phenomena. The study of parapsychology therefore gives us material for a realistic (i.e. a non-fictional) interpretation of myths, legends, fairytales, and of similar accounts. Also the phenomena seem to be much more impressive in the myths than they ever are in our laboratories, which teaches us something about the *conditions* in which strong parapsychological effects are to be expected.

Some myths even contain the relevant explanations. According to the Hopi creation myth the increasing abstraction of human thought and the increasing self-interest of man led to a drawing apart of nature and man, and the old rites which were based on harmony ceased to work as a result. Now we need not be at all surprised that our ancient ancestors were capable of inventing ideas and procedures which are potent rivals of our most advanced scientific theories. Why should they have been less intelligent than we? Stone Age man was already the fully developed *homo sapiens*, he was faced by tremendous problems, and he solved them with great ingenuity. Science is always praised because of its achievements. So, let us not forget that the inventors of myth invented fire, and the means of keeping it. They domesticated animals, bred new types of plants, kept types separate to an extent that exceeds what is possible in today's scientific agriculture. They invented rotating agriculture and developed an art that can compete with the best creations of Western man. Not being hampered by specialization they were aware of large-scale connections between man and man and man and nature which they used to improve their science and their society: the best ecological philosophy is found in the Stone Age. If science is praised because of its achievements, then myth must be praised a hundred times more fervently because its achievements were incomparably greater: the inventors of myth *started* culture while scientists just *changed* it, and not always for the better. I have already mentioned one example: myth, tragedy, the older epics dealt with emotions, facts, structures all at the same time, and they had a profound and beneficial influence on the societies in which they occurred.

The rise of Western rationalism destroyed this unity and replaced it by a more abstract, more isolated, and much more narrow idea of knowledge. Thought and emotion, even thought and nature were separated, and kept apart by fiat ('Let us build up astronomy without regard for the heavens' says Plato). One consequence which is clear to everyone who can read is that the language in which knowledge is expressed becomes impoverished, arid, formal. Another consequence is an actual drawing apart of man and nature. Of course, man eventually returns to nature, after much error he returns to nature but as her conqueror, as her enemy, not as her creature. Take a more specific example. The *Theogony* of Hesiod contains a very sophisticated and 'modern' cosmology: the world, including the laws that govern its main processes, is the result of a *development*, the laws themselves are neither eternal, nor comprehensive but come from a *dynamical equilibrium between opposing forces* so that there is always a danger of disruptive changes (the giants may break their fetters, overpower Zeus, and introduce their own laws), and the entities it contains have a twofold aspect, they are dead matter, but they are also capable of acting like things alive. These ideas were criticized as irrational by Xenophanes and Parmenides. Evolutionary accounts were replaced by explanations on the basis of eternal laws – and this lasted well into the nineteenth century! It is only now that we have returned to evolutionary theories which deal not just with restricted developments *in* the universe but with the universe as a whole and it is only now that we have realized the dynamical character of all structural arrangements. Here myth was definitely ahead of some very sophisticated, critical, and most 'rational' scientific views.

But there is more. Archaeology and especially the new discipline of astroarchaeology, combining scientific resources with a new and more realistic approach to myth has revealed the extent and the sophistication of Stone Age thought. There existed an international astronomy that was utilized and tested in observatories, taught in schools from Europe to the South Pacific, applied in international travels and codified in colourful technical language. The technical terms of this astronomy were *social* terms, *not* geometrical terms, so the science was factually adequate as well as emotionally satisfying, it solved physical as well as social problems, it provided a guide to the heavens and those harmonies between heaven and earth, matter and life, man and nature which are very real but which are overlooked or even denied by the scientific materialism of today, it was science, religion, social philosophy and poetry in one. Taking all these things together one realizes that science has no prerogative to knowledge. Science is a repository of knowledge, yes, but so are myths, fairytales, tragedies, epics and many other creations of non-scientific traditions. The knowledge contained in these traditions can be 'translated' into Western terminology, and then we obtain hypotheses of type *A*, type *B*, type *C* – but the translation omits the very important 'pragmatic' eleménts of the knowledge, it omits the way in which it is presented, the associations it evokes, and so we can judge its 'empirical content', but we cannot judge the other effects of its use, effects upon our knowledge-gathering and knowledge-improving activities included. However even in this very restricted area of empirical content we often find science limping behind some non-scientific views. Now, after this long digression, we are at last ready to look at this business of rationalism and scientific method . . .

A: And this alone is going to settle the matter! All the problems you have discussed, especially the problems of science, the problems created by the scientists' errors, by their special ideologies show that we need some standards . . .

B: . . . and these standards are supposed to be developed by philosophers and imposed on science from the outside.

A: Well, scientists only rarely consider the matter of standards and if they do they make mistakes.

B: And the philosophers don't make mistakes about standards?

A: Of course they make mistakes, but at least they are competent in the field of standards –

B: They make mistakes, but they make them competently – is that their advantage?

A: They have some insight into the complexity of the matter.

B: You are an optimist – you think philosophers of science have an inkling of the complexities of science. Why, they say themselves that they do not deal with science, they only deal with its 'rational reconstructions' and 'rational reconstructions' of science are science translated into pidgin logic.

A: They clarify science . . .

B: . . . for illiterates who understand only pidgin logic and nothing else. But I would say that if the problem is to make science clear to people of average intelligence then popularizers such as Asimov are doing a much better job. Anyone who reads Asimov knows roughly what science is about but somebody who reads Popper, or Watkins, or Lakatos will learn a rather simple-minded kind of logic but not science. Even if philosophy of science were better than it actually is, it would still share the problem of all sciences: it makes assumptions which are not easy to control and which are outside the competence of its practitioners. So adding the philosophy of science to the sciences does not remove the problems we are talking about but *adds* further problems of the same kind. The confusion becomes bigger, it does not disappear though the impression will be that it does – because of the ignorance and simple-mindedness of the philosophers.

A: Well, I admit of course that scientists and philosophers of science must be ready to learn new things.

B: How nice of you to admit this – but also how ineffective! For the very nature of the assumptions in question prevents the practitioners from learning the 'new things' that are needed to see them in perspective.

A: What do you mean?

B: Remember Atkinson?

A: How could I forget?

B: Atkinson was not prepared to give up his views of early man. His reasons: he did not understand the arguments, he 'lacked the numeracy required', if I remember his words correctly, and it was 'more comfortable' to remain in the same place. Now there are assumptions, such as the assumption that terrestrial events do not depend on planetary parameters, which are not at all as well articulated as these views, and there are further assumptions, such as the assumption that illnesses start from proximate causes, whose alternatives are not merely disbelieved but not even understood.

A: Well, what would an alternative be?

B: One possible alternative is that an illness is a structural process that is not caused by a particular event but develops as a whole out of processes of similar complexity. If that is a correct account of illness then a search for the 'location' of the illness, for the *Krankheitsherd,* is an exercise in futility and the use of scientific theories concerning such causes a hindrance.

A: How else can you proceed?

B: Your question is a good example of the effect which general assumptions of the kind I am talking about have on thinking. There are many practices one is engaged in without having learned a theory.

A: For example?

B: Speaking a language. You don't learn speaking a language by learning a theory that can be formulated explicitly, you learn it by participating in a certain practice – you pick it up. Now picking up a language enables you to do two things. It enables you to understand and to use certain *regularities* though without knowing what they are....

A: Unless you study grammar, or phonetics.

B: Unless you study grammar or phonetics. And you will also be able to understand and perhaps even imitate *idiosyncrasies*, individual variations, deviations from the norm included. You may even start introducing such deviations yourself, for example, you may become a poet and as a result change the regularities of the language you speak.

A: Yes, but a language is still a theory.

B: But it is treated in a way that is very different from the way in which philosophers of science say theories are treated.

A: Grammarians try to formulate its regularities explicitly ...

B: ... and never succeed in giving an exhaustive account, for there are too many exceptions. Besides, the formulations of the grammarians are guided by the practice of speaking the language and not the other way around. Now there are medical systems where symptoms of sickness and health are learned in the same manner in which we learn a language. The physician studies his patient until he understands the 'language of the symptoms'. This study differs radically from the study of the scientific physician who already has a theory, usually a theory taken from another domain ...

A: What do you mean: another domain?

B: The theory is not developed by generalizing from *medical* experience, it is imposed from biology, or from chemistry or even from physics.

A: But the organism is a biological system.

B: It may be, it may not be. At least the overall behaviour of an organism may not conform to the laws of biology which are suggested by non-medical experience. But this is never discovered, for having imposed biological laws on medical practice we pay attention to biological evidence and no longer to medical evidence: the domain of falsifiable facts is drastically reduced ...

A: Now you argue like a Popperian.

B: Only to make myself understood to a Popperian like you. But there is a much more important consideration and I have already mentioned it: medical evidence in the sense in which

I am discussing it now is close to the understanding of the patient – as a matter of fact the kind of doctor I am considering will often learn from the patient, he will ask him, he will regard his opinion as most important. And he must do so because he wants to make the patient healthy *in his own sense* and not in the sense of some complicated theory. I have told you that conceptions of health and sickness vary from culture to culture and from individual to individual. Healing means: restoring the state desired by the patient and not an abstract state that seems desirable from a theoretical point of view. So the kind of doctor I have in mind will maintain a close *personal* relationship with the patient not only because he is a physician and a physician should be a friend rather than a body-plumber but also because he needs personal contact to learn his craft: learning and personal relationship go hand in hand. The scientific physician, however, views the patient through the spectacles of some abstract theory; depending on the theory the patient becomes a sewer system, or a molecular aggregate, or a sack full of humours.

A: But you need a theory in order to know what is relevant and what is not.

B: I agree. But first of all the theory need not be available in explicit form ...

A: But then, how can you criticize it?

B: How do you criticize your own understanding of a language? Do you formulate a theory of grammar and test it, or do you just speak and see where it gets you?

A: The latter procedure is hardly scientific ...

B: ... assuming that science deals only with what can be formulated explicitly. But there are many hidden assumptions which need not be revealed but can be changed by simply changing our procedure. Secondly, the theories the 'scientific' physician introduces are imported from some other domain, they do not grow out of medical practice itself and so they are often irrelevant to the concerns of the practising humanitarian physician who wants to make the patients healthy in *their* sense. Now you may say that we have here two theories concerning the structure of the human body and the nature of its disturbances and so the question is which one should be preferred. Unfortunately the problem is hardly ever stated in that manner. Scientific physicians do not regard the empiricists as offering an *alternative*, they regard them as naive, unscientific incompetents ...

A: But you see, just here the philosophy of science can help a lot.

B: Are you kidding? Philosophers of science are much too busy producing technicalities of their own to have time for other things. Besides, a physician is not supposed to be scientific, he is supposed to heal.

A: But how can he heal if he has no knowledge?

B: Wounds heal all by themselves, without 'knowledge'.

A: And physicians are to act automatically, like wounds?

B: If that gets results – why not?

A: But who is to judge the result?

B: The patient, who else?

A: Then what are physicians for?

B: To aid the body in its natural processes and to aid men in their desire to live a comfortable and rewarding life – don't you see that all this discussion is beside the point? And that it is beside the point precisely because of the philosopher of science's habit of introducing his own concepts? He wants to set up a model and determine what knowledge is and what science is. He is not very successful at this activity of his – look at all the epicycles that had to be introduced to make ideas such as content increase and verisimilitude acceptable for *logicians*. The question whether they help science is never discussed – it is either taken for granted or rejected as belonging to a different field. But the activity is also irrelevant for the question we are discussing now. I have introduced two types of physicians: the scientific physician and the 'personal' physician (in the past the two groups were called Dogmatists and Empiricists and Empiricists were held in low esteem by the Dogmatists and by the philosophers). Both have certain ideas about the nature of the human organism, its functions, about the task of the physician, diagnosis, therapy, both have certain views, about the nature of knowledge. The question is: who is the better *healer*? And this question is independent of the question: who is *scientific*? It may well turn out that unscientific medicine heals and scientific medicine kills. As a matter of fact this possibility is admitted by physicians. Frans Inglefinger, Editor Emeritus of the *New England Journal of Medicine*, writes that 'although people still die in our hospitals, very few die undiagnosed': knowledge increases, content increases, patients die because scientific physicians and their uninformed defenders, the philosophers of science, prefer being 'scientific' to being humane. *And this is one of my reasons for suggesting that we take fundamental problems – epistemological problems and problems of method included – out of the hands of experts (physicians, philosophers of science, etc., etc.) and hand them over to the citizens to solve*. Experts will play an advisory role, they will be consulted, but they will not have the final say. *Citizens' initiatives instead of epistemology* – that is my slogan.

A: You mean that laymen are supposed to decide scientific matters?

B: Laymen are supposed to decide matters in their surroundings on which scientists have opinions and which are being run in accordance with the scientists' wishes.

A: This is going to create chaos.

B: Yes, I know that is what you people say for you want to keep the power over minds and pocketbooks you have stolen from the public by false pretences and false promises.

A: But people have to be protected!

B: You already said that. And I replied that they also have to be protected from scientific medicine. As a matter of fact, they have to be protected from this practice even more, for it is more dangerous than any alternative practice. Its methods of diagnosis are dangerous, its cures or so-called cures are often drastic, the accident rate at hospitals higher than at all industries, mines and high-rise construction alone excepted. 'A military officer' writes Ivan Illich on that matter, 'with a similar record of performance would be relieved of his command, and a restaurant or amusement centre would be closed by the police'. Besides, doctors come in many cases to different decisions and so it is at any rate up to the patient, or to the relatives of the patient, to make up their minds. Will they not make grievous mistakes? They will, of course they will – but their mistakes will not be bigger than those of the experts. This is shown by every trial by jury. Conceited experts give testimony; they are examined by a lawyer who is a layman in the questions discussed and it often emerges that they do not know what they are talking about. A trial by jury is an institution that decides a case with the help of experts but without letting the experts have the final say. The same arrangement should be applied to society at large for the reasons just given and additional reasons as well. People have a right to live as they see fit which means that all traditions of a society have to be given equal rights and equal access to the power centres of a society. Traditions contain not only ethical rules and religions, they also contain a cosmology, medical lore, a view about the nature of man and so on. So each tradition should be permitted to practise its own medicine, to deduct the medical expenses so incurred from the taxes, to instruct its young in the basic myth. As I said this is a basic right and the right should be implemented. Secondly the results of life in other traditions provide us with much needed information about the efficiency of science. You have said above that to check the efficiency of modern medicine one needs control groups. The difficulty is that one cannot force people to relinquish a mode of treatment they regard as important. But if traditions are given equal rights many people will choose alternative forms of medicine, psychology, sociology, etc., out of their own free will and comparative material will arise as a result. To a certain extent this procedure is being realized in the area of 'development'. Before, Western ideas of progress which meant monocultures, connection with the World Market and evaluation of results in Market terms were simply imposed. Now at least some countries discuss the nature of their 'contribution' with the local populations and proceed accordingly. Experts are no longer interposed between people and their problems. Applying this approach to the West means that problems such as the construction of bridges, use of nuclear reactors, methods to ascertain the attitude of prisoners will be decided by the citizens themselves.

A: This is certainly going to lead to lots of silly debates and ridiculous results.

B: I agree. But there will be an important difference. The debates will involve the *concerned parties*, and the ridiculous results will be results obtained and comprehended by the participants, not by a few experts shouting at each other in a language nobody understands. For don't think for a moment that the so-called results obtained by our so-called experts are less ridiculous. Just visit a conference on philosophy, or on the philosophy of science: it is hard to believe what nonsense is

nowadays produced by our 'intellectual elite' – and at the taxpayers' expense. Indeed, it is hard to believe what nonsense has been produced by the Great Men of all Ages and it is hard to understand the gullibility of the general public.
A: You don't seem to have much respect for the leaders of mankind.
B: I don't have much respect for people who either want to be leaders or permit the formation of schools producing such 'leaders'. Quite the contrary I think that many of the so-called 'educators' of mankind are just power-hungry criminals who, being dissatisfied with their own paltry selves want to reign over other minds as well and do everything in their power to increase the number of slaves. Instead of strengthening the ability of people to find their own way they use their weakness, their desire to learn, their trust so as to turn them into flesh-and-bone manifestations of their own vapid fantasies. The first duty of a teacher is to warn his audience that while he is going to tell a story which he likes and which has a nice sound to it his listeners must not be taken in. The first duty of a teacher is to tell his audience: you know much more than I do but, maybe, you will not find my account displeasing. Or he may use humour to defuse any 'intellectual impact' his story may have for it is certainly better to see people laughing than having them turned into a bunch of gaping apes.
A: You certainly don't have much respect for people.
B: Quite the contrary, I admire many people, I respect many people, but I respect only few intellectuals. I admire Marlene Dietrich who got through a long life in style and has taught a thing or two to many of us. I admire Ernst Bloch because he speaks with the tongue of the common people and enhances the colourful accounts they and their poets have given of life. I admire Paracelsus because he knew that knowledge without a heart is an empty thing. I admire Lessing for his independence, for his willingness to change his mind, I admire him even for his honesty for he is one of those very rare people who can be honest and humorous at the same time, who use their honesty as a guide for *their own private lives*, not as a club for beating people into submission, not as a showpiece for pleasing the galleries. I admire him for his style which is free, clear, vivid, very different indeed from the self-conscious and already somewhat petrified simplicity and

literacy of, say, *Objective Knowledge*. I admire him because he was a thinker without a doctrine and a scholar without a school – every problem, every phenomenon he approached was for him a unique situation that had to be explained and illuminated in a unique way. There were no boundaries for his curiosity and no 'criteria' restricted his thinking: thought and emotions, faith and knowledge were allowed to collaborate in every single investigation. I admire him because he was not satisfied with sham clarity but realized that understanding is often achieved through an *obscuring* of things, through a process in which 'what seemed to be seen clearly is lost in an uncertain distance'. I admire him because he did not reject dreams and fairytales but welcomed them as instruments for freeing mankind from the yoke of the more determined rationalists. I admire him because he was not bound to any school, to any profession, because he felt no need to check himself constantly in an intellectual mirror, like an ageing courtesan, and no desire to accumulate a 'reputation' as expressed in footnotes, acknowledgements, academic orations, honorary degrees and other medicines for the soothing of the fears of the insecure. Most of all I admire him because he never tried to gain power over his fellow men, neither by force, nor by persuasion but rested content with being 'free like a sparrow' – and equally inquisitive. So, yes, there are many people I admire, rationalists among them, rationalists like Lessing, or Heine, but not like Kant, or Popper, our own miniKant – and I am therefore an irreconcilable foe of what goes for rationalism today . . .

A: Why, my friend, what enthusiasm – I have never seen you so excited. You almost burst with religious fervour . . .

B: Never mind that – I am a sick man, and liable to go off my rocker now and then.

A: You just cannot stand being serious for more than a minute or two. Ah, well, it was certainly interesting talking to you and I hope you don't recover too soon for I prefer your sick enthusiasm to your healthy cynicism.

B: And you call yourself a rationalist!

Third Dialogue (*1989*)

Third Dialogue

A: Do you still believe in astrology?
B: Who told you I believed in astrology?
A: You yourself. Remember, when we met last time, you talked at length about astrology, faith-healing and other disreputable subjects. You were very enthusiastic about them.
B: I don't remember what I said ...
A: You don't have to remember the exact words; your position implies that ...
B: My 'position'?
A: Yes, your position, your philosophy or whatever you want to call it.
B: Who told you I had a 'philosophy'?
A: Well, I see you haven't changed much. First you make absurd statements, you condemn good ideas and praise junk, you say that this should be done and that avoided – but when somebody catches you and tries to nail you down you deny everything. 'I am Doctor Jekyll, I have done nothing.' How can anybody take you seriously?'
B: Have you ever had a friend?
A: I have many friends.
B: And you say good things about them, no doubt.
A: When I speak about them, yes.
B: Did you ever get estranged from a friend?
A: Well, I had some disappointments.
B: No, I mean something else. Did it ever happen to you that without any reason you could specify you suddenly were not

as friendly with a particular person as you used to be? Maybe you got bored of that person.
A: Well, we may have grown apart – still, I try to be rational in these matters ...
B: But you do not always succeed! Occasionally you become strangers and perhaps even a little hostile towards each other – but you can't put your finger on it.
A: In this case I certainly would try to discuss the matter with my friend – friendship is not something to be given up easily.
B: Agreed. You will talk. But will you always come to a conclusion the two of you can accept? Being estranged means that you don't understand each other very well and so the discussion may get nowhere and it may even be painful ...
A: I would not be satisfied with that ...
B: Well, you can't go on forever; at some point you will have to admit that you don't have anything to say to each other any more; then the reasonable thing is to stop and to part company.
A (*silent*).
B: I see, I have hit a nerve ...
A: Well, things like that happen; but what has this got to do with our question? With your refusal to stand by your position?
B: I'll tell you in a moment. Now take a friend from whom you are slowly becoming estranged. You meet him every day, you talk to him, or to her, there are fewer and fewer things you can discuss together, the interests you share slowly disappear, you become bored, you see signs of boredom, or of impatience on the other side, your behaviour changes – and so does what you say about your friend to others ...
A: I agree that such things happen; but when this happens I shall try to find the reasons.
B: Never mind the reasons – I am now talking about the process itself. The reason may be that your friend has come to know new people, has subtly changed his outlook, his 'tacit knowledge', the reason may be that you yourself have changed because of metabolic changes, or because you saw a powerful movie, or because you fell in love – who knows. Whatever the reason for the change, you now act differently towards each other and, more importantly, you think and speak differently about each other.

A: Now I know what you are up to! What you want to say is that your relation to the world and to its physical and social aspects changes just as the relation between two people changes ...

B: Precisely. In 1970, when I wrote the first version of *Against Method*, the world was different from what it is now and I was different from what I am now, not only intellectually but also emotionally ...

A: But that was not the point of my remark. I did not criticize you for having changed your philosophy, or your position. I criticized you for either having no position at all or for drifting around from one position to the next, just as the mood strikes you. Today you defend astrology, tomorrow your tastes change and you praise molecular biology ...

B: Not bloody likely ...

A: Anyway. Let us admit that there are lots of changes going on in our surroundings. The weather changes, there are large-scale changes like from the Ice Age to a warmer climate, small-scale changes like from a rainy day to a day with sunshine, people discover new forms of mathematics – there is change all over the place. But rationalists do not just drift in this ocean of change, they try to adapt their own changes to those around them ...

B: You mean they have theories which they adapt to new facts and to new mathematical forms ...

A: Yes. Now the case of two people is a little more complex and not different in principle.

B: And by this you mean that I can in principle separate my change from that of my friend and give an objective account of the latter.

A: Yes.

B: For example, going into details, I could say that right now he 'objectively' might have a friendly smile on his face, no matter if anyone is looking or not.

A: Yes.

B: But you no doubt know that the same face, incorporated into different stories, can be read in very different ways.

A: What do you mean?

B: Assume you have the drawing of a smiling face. Now incorporate it into a text that says: '... at last he held the little creature in his arms – his son. His only son! He looked at him

tenderly and smiled ...' – well, the reader will 'read' the drawing as the drawing of a person with a tender smile on his face.
A: And?
B: Next put the same drawing into the following text: '... at last he had his enemy cringeing at his feet and begging for mercy. He bowed down to him with a cruel smile and said ...' – in which case 'the same' drawing will be read as expressing a cruel smile. A face, after all, can be read in many different ways and can appear in many different ways, dependent on the situation ...
A: But ...
B: A moment. Let me give you a few more examples! Long ago I was madly in love with a Jugoslavian lady – a former Olympic champion.
A: I have heard about your adventures.
B: Vicious gossip, no doubt! Well, when the affair began I was 28 and she was 40. We stayed together for a few years and then we parted. I went to England, then to the USA. When she was about 60 I visited her. I rang the doorbell, the door opened and there was a plump little greyhaired lady. 'Aha,' I said 'she's got a housekeeper' – but it was her and as soon as I realized that, her face changed and became the younger face I remembered. Another example: in the USA I got married to a lady much younger than me – a very attractive lady. The marriage did not go well.
B: Your fault, no doubt!
A: I don't think it was anybody's fault although I agree that I am a difficult person to live with. At any rate – after some time she did not look so beautiful any more. One fine day I went to the library to browse in the journal section and there, in the distance, I saw a very attractive lady. Naturally I approached her – but it was my wife and the moment I realized that, she changed and her face became just an ordinary face.
A: Like Don Giovanni and Donna Elvira ...
B: Right! That is an excellent comparison! A third example. Some years ago I was walking towards a wall and saw a very disreputable individual coming towards me. 'Who is that bum?' I asked myself – and then I discovered that the wall was in fact a mirror and that I had been looking at myself. At once

the bum turned into an elegant and intelligent-looking character. So, you see, you simply cannot speak of an 'objective' smile of a person and, as human relations are composed of smiles, gestures, feelings, 'objective' friendship is just as impossible a notion as inherent bigness: things are big and small *relative to* other things, not in themselves. A smile is a smile *for an observer*, not in and for itself.
A: But relations can be objective – the theory of relativity shows that ...
B: Not if the elements between which the relation obtains are involved in a historical process that produces novel events! In this case we can describe a particular stage of the relation; we cannot generalize, for there is no permanent substratum containing permanent and objectivizable features. Just look at the history of portraiture in the West, from archaic Greece up to, say, Picasso, Kokoschka and modern photographers. And don't make the mistake of assuming that these pictures reveal what people saw when looking at other people – the few stories I told you make it clear, at least to me, that I shall never know how you see me, how I see myself, and I shall therefore never know who I 'really' am, or, for that matter, who anybody 'really' is. As far as I am concerned, all attempts at self-identification only succeed in freezing a certain aspect, they don't reveal an aspect-independent 'reality'. Pirandello often talks about such matters, for example, in his *Enrico IV*: 'I would not wish you to think, as I have done, about this horrible situation which really drives one mad: that if you were beside another, and looking into his eyes – as I one day looked into somebody's eyes – you might as well be a beggar before a door never to be opened to you: for he who does enter there will never be you, but someone unknown to you with his own different and impenetrable world.' So all you can do is report your impressions, surround your report with a few comments and hope for the best.
A: But this is absurd.
B: Of course it is! We are living in an absurd world!
A: Wait a minute! Wait a minute! We are *talking* about these matters and we *come to conclusions*. Let's take an actor – you seem to like actors.
B: I certainly do. They *create* illusions and they *know* it while your average philosopher, knowing much less about the art of

makeup – intellectual makeup, in his case – *suffers from* the illusion of having found 'the Truth'.
A: Well, I obviously don't agree with you – but I don't want to argue the case. What I do want to say is that your remark refutes your assumption of absurdity. An actor creates an illusion, you say. How does he proceed? He starts with a general idea of the character he is going to play, he thinks about details such as gestures, the way in which the character walks, his idiosyncrasies of speech; he uses makeup very carefully to get the face right. He has an aim, a procedure, and a way of judging the results. Judges, advocates, plaintiffs, defendants do what they do and say what they say because they recognize what is going on; you respond to what I say in a certain way because you think that your comments will unsettle me, or draw me over to your side ...
B: Nothing could be further from my mind! I don't have a 'side' and if I had, I would not like it to be crowded with strangers ...
A (*as if he had not heard*): ... at any rate, there is understanding, though never complete understanding, there is agreement, or disagreement, though the matter is never certain, and now you want to suggest that all this is built on sand.
B: But it is! You argue from the simplicity of the process to the simplicity and comprehensibility of the elements involved ...
A: I would not say that the process is simple – it may take months before an actor gets the right ideas and their right physical embodiment, and the preparations for a trial take years!
B: Granted – it may take months and even years! But there is some agreement about the steps, the actor can explain his aims to others, and conclusions are reached. This is what you just said. What *I* say is that the elements that enter the process vary from one participant to the next and they vary in a way that is beyond control and insight. A debate, therefore, is not like a journey on a clearly recognizable road; every part of the road can turn out to be a chimaera and even if it is not, even if there is solid ground beneath you and others, you are not at all sure that this is not a dream or, worse, that you are not talking in your sleep while the others assume you are wide awake and respond to your fantasies.

A: You certainly have very strange views – I don't even know where to begin!
B: Just leave it at that: *I* see a series of miracles where *you* see a fairly orderly progression from one thought or action to the next.
A: Now if I understand you correctly you not only say that this happens *occasionally*, you say it happens all the time, hence all you can do is report your impressions and hope for the best.
B: You got it.
A: Then people are justified in not taking you seriously.
B: And by 'people' you mean philosophers, I presume?
A: And sociologists, and just every rational being.
B: Poets also?
A: You think you are a poet?
B: I wish I had the talent – but look: there are many people who report their impressions in poems, plays, pictures, novels – and they are not only being read, they have something to offer, we can learn from them, we can learn from the way the world appears to them ...
A: But you just said that there are only illusions and miracles!
B: Did I say that? Then I expressed myself badly. After all, speaking of illusions assumes some kind of 'reality'. But I did say that miracles are spread all over the place, and that learning is one of them.
A: Then let us forget about the miracles and just talk in a straightforward manner, as everybody does – and if we do that, then I have to criticize you for trying to get information from the wrong source ...
B: The wrong source?
A: Plays, pictures, poems belong to the arts; they have very little to do with knowledge.
B: That's what *you* say. But why should I accept your way of subdividing the things people do? Considering, for example, that great wisdom is contained in Plato's dialogues, Chuang-tse's stories, Tolstoy's novels, Brecht's poems. Did you ever read Brecht's poem 'To those who are born after us'? It reports an impression. But what a powerful lesson we can draw from it!
A: You conflate all categories. Of course, I admit there is

wisdom in these stories, dialogues, novels, but rational knowledge ...

B: There you go again with your subdivisions! Wisdom as opposed to 'rational knowledge' ...

A: But there *is* a real distinction here! As a matter of fact, the first philosophers in the West introduced this distinction because they wanted to replace poetry, by which they meant Homer, with something better. Poets, they said, tell falsehoods, they rouse the emotions, they do not prepare people for their work as responsible citizens.

B: Which proves my point! Chuangtse, Homer, Hesiod on the one side and Heraclitus, Parmenides etc. on the other are not just doing different things, they compete with each other. Plato himself speaks of the 'old quarrel between philosophy and poetry'. Both sides provide pictures of the world and the role of humans in it, but the poetic picture is blurred and falsely drawn, according to the philosophers. And now my question is: is the philosophical picture and its offspring, the scientific picture with its abstract concepts and its strict laws, so much better, are the instruments of wisdom that developed out of the rationalism of Parmenides, Plato, Aristotle, Kant etc. so much more satisfying than the instruments of wisdom provided by Brecht, or Tolstoy, that we can disregard the latter?

A: But we don't disregard them! They are still here, they are flourishing, they are taught at our schools ...

B: Yes; they are still here; and they are being taught. But they are assigned to a special category! They are called 'arts', the theory (i.e. the account provided by the rational category) being that while 'rational' thought produces 'objective' information, the arts do not. Knowledge is not their business. In psychology courses you read about experiments and theories, you do not read Turgenev.

A: Well, there certainly is no artist who could replace the work of our modern particle physicists.

B: You cannot generalize from extreme cases ...

A: But did you not do exactly that? Trying to spread the arts all over the domain of knowledge?

B: No, by no means. What I meant was that the arts contain *some* knowledge and not, that for *every* piece of information that comes out of the sciences there exists a corresponding *and equally weighty* piece of information in the arts. Why – that is not even true of the sciences! For example, not every discovery made in one area of science can at once be duplicated or improved in another area that competes with it. Transposition and irreversibility were discovered by phenomenological methods and it took time and much thought before a micro-account became available. In some ways the matter of irreversibility is not solved, not even today – but there is still the second law of the phenomenological theory! Occasionally the situation is reversed: an area low on the ladder of authority produces estimates that contradict the estimates made in an area high on the ladder of authority – and the 'unimportant' estimate turns out to be right. The debate between geologists and astronomers about the correct time scale (long vs. short) during the last century belongs to this category. On the other hand, psychologists, ecologists, human relations experts can learn a lot from poets, novelists, actors such as Stanislavsky, dramatists such as Aeschylus, Lessing or Brecht, even from Beckett, though that guy is not at all my favourite. Chuangtse tells the following story:

> The Emperor of the South was called Shu and the Emperor of the North, Hu [each meaning 'very fast' and both together 'in a flash']. The Emperor of the Centre was known as Hun-t'un [chaos]. One time the Emperors of the South and the North visited Hun-t'un's territories, where they met with him. Hun-t'un made them heartily welcome. Shu and Hu conferred together as to how they could show their gratitude. They said: 'All men have seven apertures – the eyes, the ears, the mouth, and the nose – whereby they see, hear, eat and breathe. Yet this Hun-t'un, unlike other men, is quite smooth with no apertures at all. He must find it very awkward. As a sign of gratitude, therefore, let us try making some holes for him.' So each day they made a fresh hole; and on the seventh day Hun-t'un died.

Is this not an excellent analogy for colonization and some aspects of 'development' – except that the motive force here was not gratitude but presumption and greed.

A: I don't see the connection at all.

B: Well, not everybody reacts to a story in the same way. I myself reacted strongly and saw the connection at once.

A: Which means that we are dealing with subjective impressions and not with knowledge!
B: Call it what you will – the process plays an important role, even in the sciences.
A: I don't believe it!
B: Have you heard of superstrings, and of the so-called 'Theory of Everything'?
A: I have heard the words – but I have no idea what the theory is all about.
B: Well, it is an attempt, and some people say a very successful attempt, to derive the properties of space, time and matter from a single fundamental theory. The theory is not complete, for example, it has nothing to say about the known masses of elementary particles; but there exist some very interesting results. In the minds of many physicists it is only a matter of time before details emerge. However there are other physicists who call the theory 'crazy and in the wrong direction'. Richard Feynman, in an interview on BBC that was published in a very interesting little booklet (*Superstrings*, P. C. W. Davies and J. Brown, eds, Cambridge University Press, 1988 – the passage occurs on page 194), had the following to say: 'I don't like that they are not calculating anything. I don't like that they don't check their ideas. I don't like that for anything that disagrees with experiment, they cook up an explanation – a fix-up to say "Well, it might still be true" ...' and so on.
A: Well, isn't that a valid criticism?
B: Yes and no! No theory is ever complete; every theory can do with some improvements, as every story can. Moreover, in the early stages a theory faces many conflicting facts and, mind you, these 'early stages' can last months, years and even centuries.
A: Centuries? Do you have an example, or are you exaggerating as usual?
B: No, I do have an example: the behaviour of Jupiter and Saturn seemed beyond the reach of Newton's theory until Laplace found the solution. Newton knew of the discrepancy and used it as an argument in favour of divine interference. I have an even better example: the atomic theory was conceived in antiquity, in the fifth century BC, it was refuted by Aristotle ...
A: Aristotle refuted atomism?

B: He had excellent arguments against it, arguments taken partly from commonsense, partly from the physics of his time. And he was by no means the last writer to argue against atoms; scientists argued against atomism as late as the nineteenth century. Still, some people, some very intelligent people, continued working on it.
A: Maybe atomism was successful.
B: It was, to a certain extent; but so were its alternatives. On the other hand, atomism suffered from many difficulties, both of an empirical and of a formal nature. Thus the scientists who chose atomism either acted in a completely irrational fashion and were lucky nevertheless – which would show that it pays to be irrational – or they were convinced by arguments of a non-empirical and non-formal kind, in short, they were convinced by what many people call metaphysical considerations. In both cases they can be aided by stories, different scientists using different stories as their support: if they are 'irrational', then they will pick up the story that pleases them most and follow its lead. If they want to argue, then they will still pick up some story and extract from it a lesson that remains lost to others. For Yukawa, who predicted the pi-meson, the story I told above was a wonderful simile of the situation at the elementary particle level.
A: I think you draw the wrong conclusion from some obvious facts. Scientists have to eat; therefore food plays a role in their research. However I would not say that it enters research, or is an element of research. In the same way your story may play a role in scientific research ...
B: Wait a minute, be careful – trying to keep science rational you make it more irrational ...
A: What do you mean?
B: I introduced stories because stories consist of words and we argue through words. Putting stories on the same level as food, or sleep, you imply that important scientific decisions and large areas of research are beyond the reach of argument or, to use your favourite invective, you imply that they are irrational.
A: I don't follow you.
B: Remember, we are talking about a situation in which a scientist either chooses one of two empirically inadequate and formally unsatisfactory theories or prefers an empirically

inadequate and formally unsatisfactory conjecture to a good and well-established theory. Now in such a situation we can either say that the choice is irrational, or we can say that there are reasons for the choice, though the reasons obviously will be neither empirical nor formal – or 'scientific', as some people are in the habit of saying. Now take your pick. Do you want to say that scientists who choose in such a situation have no reasons but are just following a whim?

A: It would be nice if one could show that they had reasons.

B: But what kind of reasons would they be? The formulae are faulty, the evidence is hostile – scientists know that. Yet they hope that they will succeed. This means that they have (a) a view that differs both from their formulae and from the lesson of the evidence and that they have (b) a prophecy concerning the history of this view. They also need, (c), some ideas about how to examine the view, for example they need ideas about how much conflict with the evidence and how much internal incoherence they are going to tolerate. In other words, they have a metaphysics, a prophecy and a style of research. Now prophecies, metaphysical views and styles can be argued about – but the arguments are not binding. Feynman wants research to be closely controlled by facts and mathematics. That is one style, based on one metaphysics. Superstringers are prepared to wander off into the blue yonder and expect to find treasures there – that is another style, based on another metaphysics. It is like different stories, being comprehensible to different people and providing them with arguments for different things.

A: You mean the stories are incommensurable?

B: Not at all; given time the opponents might well be able to explain matters to each other – however, right now the explanation is missing and the stories are not understood; that's all there is to it and it occurs in the sciences, in politics; as a matter of fact, it occurs everywhere.

A: Still, I am not happy about your story by Chuangtse. I try to understand what it might mean – assume I do; assume I really see some connection with development. I would still say that it just spreads the fog of emotion over the whole situation.

B: Dear God, protect us from rationalist rhetoric! The story may indeed spread emotion over the whole situation, but this clarifies the situation, it does not cover it with a fog. Emotions and stories with an emotional impact are forceful instruments for creating a new *and clear* perspective. A developer may think he does lots of good; now he reads the story – and suddenly things look very different. Remember the case of the microscope we discussed over ten years ago?

A: I am not sure ...

B: Well, I told you, and you agreed, that a novice looking into a microscope may not see anything definite, just a chaos of structures and motions. He has read textbooks, he has seen wonderful drawings of interesting creatures, but he does not find these creatures anywhere in his field of vision. He has to learn seeing things in a new way. And I also told you that the early reluctance to accept Galileo's telescopic observations can at least in part be explained by the same phenomenon. Now in the social field – and that includes scientific communication – we don't have telescopes, or microscopes, we just have our instincts, beliefs, our alleged knowledge and our perceptions. Strong emotions may change them and make us see things in a different light. What I want to say is that Chuangtse's story can have the same function as instruction in microscopic vision. Sociologists, in their eagerness to imitate what they think is proper scientific procedure, remove all these 'subjective' means of instruction and thus blind themselves and others to important aspects of the world; trying to be 'objective' they end up in subjective prisons. Why, even physicists have learned from Chuangtse. Yukawa, whom I already mentioned, writes: 'It is likely that the most basic thing of all has no fixed form and corresponds to none of the elementary particles we know at present.' Later on he says: 'Books make their appeal in many different ways, but I am particularly fond of the kind of work that creates a world of its own in which, if only for a short time, it succeeds in immersing the reader.' Having immersed himself the reader emerges as a different person with a different relation to the world around him and different ideas about it – precisely the kind of development that occurs when two people meet, become acquainted, become friends, and turn into strangers again. Besides, some parts of physics are now going through changes that considerably decrease the distance between the arts, the humanities and the sciences and more recent studies in the history of the sciences show that the friendship story, interpreted historically, and not 'objectively', is not at all that far-fetched.

A: What are you talking about?

B: Historians have studied the actual sequence of the events that lead from a scientific problem to a conjecture to phenomenological calculations to the acquisition of equipment, the preparation of an experiment, the trial runs, the evaluation of the data, the projection of results and the final acceptance of the results not by all scientists, but by almost all members of the small group that is closely acquainted with the problem (the rest then accepts or contests the results on very different grounds). Historians have studied this sequence by using letters, computer printouts, records of business transactions (very important today when experiments involve entire cities of people), reports of meetings, diaries and personal interviews and not only the finished products, i.e. papers or biographies, as did the older historians. Proceeding in this way they discovered that the process contains much that is tentative, not explicit, as a matter of fact it contains much of what happens when two people become friendly, detached, estranged.

A: Which is exactly what Popper says. He says that when dealing with a problem we make conjectures, that the conjectures are tentative, that we revise them on the basis of refutations ...

B: Which is exactly what does *not* happen at decisive junctures of scientific research. Conjectures there may be, but many of them are unconscious and they are changed and modified without any explicit discussion, simply as part of an overall process of adaptation. And note, the adaptation does not involve a mystical entity, called 'objective reality', but real relations between people and things. It involves colleagues, moneybags, financial restrictions, limitations of time, the ever-changing ocean of mathematic formalisms, the judgement of distant supervising panels, the capacity of data processors, magnets etc. etc. Even politics plays a role (CERN is financed on the basis of political agreements between various countries and proposals are accepted or rejected under the influence of all sorts of attempts at increasing national prestige). Phenomena analogous to the change of a smile from a kind smile to a cruel smile occur at all stages of this process and they keep it going. When experiments were still small-scale the 'personal' relation of the experimenter to his equipment played an important role – read Holton on the Millikan–Ehrenhaft dispute. The experimenter 'knew' his equipment. Part of the knowledge could be written down, a large part was intuitive, it was the result of a learning process that had much in common with the way one learns to dance, to drive a car, to speak a language, to get along with a difficult person. Read Michael Polanyi on 'tacit knowledge'. Today the situation is further complicated by the existence of large-scale equipment and research teams. Peter Galison wrote a very interesting book, *The Way Experiments End*, which shows how false, how completely illusionary the older 'rational reconstructions' are. Read this book. All you can do, if you really want to be truthful, is *to tell a story*, a story that contains non-repeatable elements side by side with vague analogies to other stories in the field or in distant fields. Now philosophers (and also some scientists) are accustomed to elevating analogies into principles and to claim (1) that these principles underlie all reasoning, (2) that they are responsible for the successes of science and (3) that science, therefore, deserves a central position in our culture. (1) and (2) are false and so is (3), the result inferred from them.

A: Do you mean to deny that there are theories and that different experimenters and theoreticians working in different fields often use the same theory in their research?

B: I don't deny that at all – but the question is: what is it that remains the same? There may be the same formulae (though even that is not always true – this is why many papers and textbooks use a table of symbols at the end) – but they are certainly employed in very different ways. Newton's theory as presented in the *Principia* had little to do with the calculation of perturbations Newton produced later on, both differed from the mechanics of the eighteenth and nineteenth centuries (the formula *Force equals Mass times Acceleration* is not found anywhere in Newton) and these theories differed again from the 'classical mechanics' of relativists and quantum theoreticians. What we have is a story which has a certain core but is transformed in many ways, depending on the historical situations created by (a) new discoveries in mathematics, (b) new observational results, (c) new ideas about the 'nature of knowledge'. Modern elementary particle physics is a fascinating obstacle race on a course defined by a few general principles and an ever-changing arrangement of special assumptions, facts, mathematical instruments, etc., etc. The general theory of relativity that figures in the 'Theory of Everything' is not the general theory of relativity as presented by Einstein in 1919, etc., etc. Wherever we look we find complex historical developments with certain overlaps – nothing more. I admit that the friendship example I used at the beginning is somewhat simplistic, but I think it catches important features of the process and this is all I need. The social sciences are even closer to my example – as a matter of fact, I would say that my example provides a paradigm of the social sciences that is much more realistic than the theories that are now floating around in this area. Some social scientists have realized this and tell stories instead of proposing theories. An example is Paul Starr's wonderful book *The Social Transformation of American Medicine* (Basic Books, New York, 1982) – which was duly criticized by the theory-freaks for being 'unscientific', 'episodic', etc., etc. Well, 'episodic' it is – but what must be added is that the only true accounts are episodic accounts ...

A: So you are against theories?

B: No, I am not against theories, I am against a Platonistic interpretation of theories that views them as descriptions of permanent features of the universe.

A: But there must be some permanent features ...

B: 'There must be' is the excuse used by people who have no arguments ...

A: What about planetary astronomy? What about the great successes of the theory of relativity? What about the space programme?

B: What about them?

A: These are certainly successes.

B: Yes, they are successes – but successes of what? Aristophanes was a great success with ancient audiences. He correctly gauged their mood, the way they would react to images, lines, characters, and he won prizes. His earlier plays are different from his later plays, partly because he developed and partly because his audience developed. Scientists, I claim, do the same.

A: But scientists have theories ...

B: They are aware of regularities, just as Aristophanes was – he knew the regularities of the Greek language. Scientists, in addition to being aware of regularities, formulate them and test the formulations, at least at some stages of their research. Aristophanes did not formulate the regularities he knew, he was not a grammarian, but he tested them by changing things a little bit here and a little bit there and bringing the result before a large audience. This is exactly the way in which an anthropologist proceeds who invades and studies a hitherto unexamined group of people. He does this, he does that – he may get killed, as William Jones was by the Ilongot, he may survive and be able to write a book as did Michelle Rosaldo (also about the Ilongot) in her *Knowledge and Passion* (Cambridge, 1980). The difference between Aristophanes and an anthropologist is that (a) Aristophanes did not formulate the results of his trials in abstract terms, (b) he reported to the very people he had studied and (c) he tried to instruct as well as to entertain – as a matter of fact, the two things are inextricably tied together in his work (it is different with Brecht who is much more theoretical). 'Scientific' anthropologists, on the other hand, do not regard their ability to move around in a tribe and, perhaps, to please the people of the tribe by doing useful or entertaining things, they do not regard this ability as knowledge. They study people not as friends (though they may use the appearance of friendship as a methodological device) but as parasites, as intellectual parasites, but as parasites nevertheless. And they are not satisfied with their newly acquired abilities – they have to bring these abilities into the proper form: there have to be 'data' and 'classifications', the 'data' have to be 'objective' – and so on. And so they finally tell a story no indigenous person is likely to understand though it is a story not only about them, but about the way in which an initially ignorant stranger experienced their life. Using abstract categories we might say that the anthropologist transforms impressions into knowledge – but saying that we at once realize how culture-dependent this so-called 'knowledge' really is. I have also the feeling that while Aristophanes was a humanitarian, an anthropologist, as I described him, is not. Just read Malinowski's diaries! Let me add in all fairness that not all anthropologists proceed in this way, that there are now great changes in the field and that Rosaldo, for example, is very clear about the difference between scientific data and human experience ...

A: But all this has nothing to do with our discussion. I agree that the regularities some sociologists come up with and present in highly abstract terms are not laws but passing historical features and that their formulation may hide this property. But there are laws of nature and they do not change. Besides, having denied any difference between the sciences and the arts you now introduce one yourself: the artist uses his knowledge to act on those the knowledge is about, the anthropologist uses knowledge to satisfy the idle curiosity of strangers. And one more thing – all you said so far only shows that what some people call artistic activity – and what you exemplify by the story of the two friends – *plays a role* in the sciences, and not that *all of science* is like that. But everybody acknowledges this by now! Remember the distinction between a context of discovery and a context of justification. Discovery, everybody admits, may be irrational, full of personal elements, 'artistic'. But what you have discovered in this irrational way is then subjected to a test – and this test imposes severe standards, it is objective and no longer depends on personal elements.

B: I did not deny that you can draw lines between activities. What I do deny is that there exists *one big line* with all the sciences on one side and all the arts on the other. As regards the matter of discovery and justification – I already gave my answer when I talked about experiments: the process of accepting the results of an experiment is shot through with personal elements and group idiosyncrasies just as the process of discovery is. As a matter of fact – the dichotomy discovery/justification is quite unreal. 'Discovery' is never a mere leap into the dark, or a dream; lots of reasoning enters into it. And 'justification' is never a completely 'objective' procedure – there are many personal elements. I agree with Galison that the social component of this process has occasionally been exaggerated – professional prejudices play at least a comparable role – but it is there and adds to the complexity of the process. Now, as regards physics, I agree of course that there are regularities and that physicists have succeeded in finding them and formulating them. But I would add that the process that leads up to accepting a particular statement as the expression of a regularity has much in common with what Aristophanes was doing, though the ways in which both scientists and philosophers described it so far suggest a very different, much simpler and much more 'rigorous' procedure. Also planets are not people, so the situation is simpler *because of the objects of discourse* and not because we have moved from 'knowledge' into a different field. If I were as fond of generalities as you are I would say that the old distinction between the physical sciences and the social sciences (including the humanities) is a distinction without a corresponding difference – all sciences are humanities and all humanities contain knowledge. Of course, there is a great difference between the appearance of a physical theory and the appearance of a story about King Henry VIII. But 'subjectivity' and 'objectivity' mix equally in both domains and the case of the two friends turns up everywhere. Indeed, without 'understanding' their equipment in the sense in which some historians claim they 'understand' a distant historical figure scientists would not get anywhere. Today we can say even more. The speculations connected with superstrings, twistors, alternative universes no longer consist in formulating assumptions and then testing them, they are much more like developing a language that satisfies certain very general constraints (though it need not satisfy them slavishly) and then constructing a convincing and beautiful story in terms of this language. It is really very much like writing a poem. Poems are not without constraints. As a matter of fact, the constraints poets impose on their work are often much more severe than the constraints accepted by a botanist, or a birdwatcher. Read Milman Parry on Homer. Again the constraints are not obeyed slavishly and there must be a vague connection with the world as we know it. Twistor theory or superstring theory uses mathematical formulae – that is the only difference.

A: But they cover everything while a poem just covers a passing mood.

B: What do you mean by 'they cover everything'?

A: Well, are not the theories developed on the basis of the speculations you just described called 'Theories of Everything'? You said so yourself!

B: Don't be misled by a word! 'Everything' means: special

relatively, general relativity, subatomic particle classifications, electro-weak and strong-force gauge theories, supersymmetry and supergravity.
A: And as everything consists of elementary particles arranged in space and time these theories, once they succeed, really cover everything there is.
B: Boy, are you naive! First of all, these theories so far describe not our present situation but, possibly, a situation that existed during the first few moments after the Big Bang. There is no prediction of the particle masses as we know them, as a matter of fact there is very little in terms of concrete predictions. Secondly, even a complete account of elementary particles does not yet give us small molecules, or large molecules, or solid bodies, or living things.
A: But has not molecular biology gone a long way in reducing biology to molecular science?
B: Let's be a little more modest: has chemistry succeeded in reducing molecules to elementary particles? Only if by reduction you mean something that involves subtracting some kind of information and replacing it by information of a different kind. Elementary particle processes have a feature of wholeness, you cannot describe the behaviour of a collection of elementary particles by postulating separate particles and fields between them.
A: Has this something to do with complementarity?
B: Yes it has.
A: But complementarity has been refuted long ago!
B: By whom?
A: By Einstein.
B: Where?
A: In his argument of Einstein, Podolskiy and Rosen.
B: Well, that is the interesting thing about the matter. The argument was supposed to refute complementarity but only succeeded in establishing it more firmly.
A: How?
B: You know that the argument is based on the assumption that what you do to one particle does not affect a particle that once interacted with it but is now far away?
A: Yes.
B: The assumption was tested and found to be incorrect.
A: Can you tell me more about it?

B: That would take too long – but the matter is connected with a theorem by Bell and various tests of that theorem. There are still some difficulties but as of now the matter seems to be clear: the assumption is incorrect.

A: And?

B: Well, that means that there exist correlations between distant particles which make it impossible to regard them as separate entities. On the other hand, regarding things as separate entities means neglecting effects that do exist but do not show up when you look at things in a certain way. Regarding things as separate entities means, therefore, adopting a point of view or, to speak differently, molecules are not 'objective', they are *what appears* when we proceed in a certain way – and now we have to specify the way, i.e. we have to specify the overall conditions of chemical research – and *that* specification is *not* contained in the basic theories. Symmetries are broken, new properties appear which cannot be derived from the basic theory. One might say that the basic theories are schemata whose details have to be filled in to give concrete predictions but which do not describe anything that exists independently of the details. The details include specifications of the approach used, i.e. they include information about the special physical conditions of the observer.

A: Molecular biologists do not speak in that way.

B: You are right – they speak like the ancient atomists, the only difference being that their 'atoms' have become very complex. But they also assert that what they say is supported by the quantum theory – and here they are wrong. Hans Primas, Professor of Physical Chemistry at the Federal Institute of Technology in Zürich, where I have a job and am paid in solid Swiss Francs, has made this very clear. Read his wonderful book *Chemistry, Quantum Mechanics and Reductionism* (Springer, New York, 1984). The idea of objectivity which seems to be behind many of your arguments is also endangered by other developments, for example by considerations in connection with the so-called anthropic principle. We have now some theories about the origin of life and of the elements. There was a Big Bang, then original symmetries were broken, bosons were separated from fermions, hydrogen and helium arose, there were big aggregations, smaller aggregations, fixed stars, and it is here that the elements arose, especially carbon which is essential for life. Now a very slight change in familiar constants, e.g. a very slight change in the relation between the mass of the proton and the mass of the neutron, leads to a radically different development with no life anywhere. This means that the laws we find are those of a universe in which we can live, or, as Hawking expressed it, 'Things are as they are because we are'.

A: Well, I would have to look at the whole thing in greater detail.

B: I can't follow all the details either – but let us talk about something we can follow. Your 'Theory of Everything' – it certainly does not talk about love, or disappointment, or sadness ...

A: But these are subjective events ...

B: They are there, whatever you call them, and they are beyond the reach of the most sophisticated physical or biological theory. However, they are not beyond the reach of artists, painters, poets, writers of plays. Now love, disappointment, desire play a large role in the lives of people. They also play a role in the process of scientific research, as I said a little earlier. Hence, if you really want to understand the sciences and not merely write dry and abstract fairytales about them – and remember, by 'understanding the sciences' I mean both the context of discovery and the context of justification – then you have to turn to the arts and the humanities, i.e. you have to abandon these artificial classifications most philosophies and 'rational accounts' are full of. A really comprehensive world view absolutely cannot do without the poets ...

A: Did you say: a really comprehensive world view?

B: Yes – but I don't mean a *theory*, I mean an attitude of mind, partly expressible in words, partly in actions such as making music, writing down equations, loving, painting, eating, talking to other people, that can make sense of many things, i.e. can explain them to others ...

A (*opens his mouth*).

B: I know what you want to say – you want to say that before explaining something to others we need a theory of explanation or a clear concept of explanation. This is not true! 'Explaining something to others' is a complicated process that has lots of false starts and ends with some kind of harmony,

and the kind of harmony it ends with cannot be anticipated, but will be recognized when it comes ...
A: But how can it be recognized when we do not know what it is?
B: You assume that an experience cannot arise unless we have a notion of it. That is a very unrealistic assumption. It would mean that we can never experience anything fundamentally new. I think it is this assumption that lies behind your criticism at the beginning.
A: What criticism?
B: You already forgot? Your criticism that I cannot be taken seriously because, when taken to task for my 'position', I say I have no position. Well, in a sense I do and in a sense I don't. I do have a position in the sense that I react to things in certain ways. I don't have a position in the sense that my reactions cannot be tied to universal principles and stable meanings.
A: So you are not a relativist?
B: There you are! You throw a word at me that has lots of associations tied to it and expect me to say yes or no.
A: Well, do you think that there are universal principles of reasoning?
B: The matter is not that simple.
A: God in heaven help me!
B: Be patient and listen! Here I have three statements:

> Cotton needs a hot and dry climate.
> England is cold and damp.
> Cotton does not grow in England.

Does the third statement follow from the first two?
A: Obviously.
B: And to say this you have to realize that there exists a certain relation between the first two statements and the third?
A: Obviously.
B: And you would agree that there are people who do not realize this, i.e. who take the statements one by one?
A: Well, there are always idiots around!
B: Don't be so fast! Can you imagine a situation in which it

would be of advantage to take statements one by one and not to be sidetracked into considering their mutual relations?
A: This would have to be a very simple world!
B: Simple or not – can you imagine such a situation?
A (*looks puzzled*).
B: Let me take another example: look at the drawings below.

Are they like each other or are they unlike?
A: They certainly are alike – they are circular!
B: Good. Now what would you say if I told you that in psychological tests carried out with illiterate people in Uzbekistan in the thirties the three things were regarded as utterly different from each other – the first was classified as a bracelet, the second as the moon and the third as a coin.
A: Who made these experiments?
B: You can read about them in A. R. Luria's autobiography, *The Making of Mind* (Harvard University Press, 1979), chapter 4.
A: Well, these people had not learned to abstract the shape from a drawing.
B: You think that is a disadvantage?
A: Certainly.
B: But think now – these people are not mathematicians, or engineers looking at blueprints – they are peasants and huntsmen who have to recognize objects from indistinct clues. All their perception is object-directed and necessarily so, to fit their way of life. They not only don't need abstraction, it would hinder them.
A: Well, for their way of life.
B: Exactly – for their way of life.
A: But their life can be improved.
B: That is a different problem. As long as they live in this way – this is the right kind of perception to have. Now, let's move on to the above example of logic. In practical life you often take things one by one. You ask yourself: is it so? is it not so? what do I know about it? – and that is that.
A (*hesitatingly*): Agreed.

B: And comparing statements would slow up this process.
A: It would have other benefits.
B: The important thing is that *there are benefits* in not proceeding in this way, i.e. in not recognizing 'logical relations'. It's not just a matter of idiocy. And then there is a choice – what do you prefer? Can you have both? And so on. Now I can well imagine that there are beings for whom considering the relation of statements to each other completely paralyses everyday life. Do you think that in this case it makes much sense to speak of 'universal and objective principles of reasoning'?
A: But humans are not like that!
B: Precisely – *for humans* it is useful to consider these relations; that is all we can say. And we can abbreviate it by saying that they are 'objective' relations bearing in mind that the choice of a certain way of living is involved and not a Platonic pattern.
A: So you *are* a relativist.
B: In a way, yes. But I have great difficulties with some forms of relativism. According to some forms of relativism whatever one says is valid only 'within a certain system'. This assumes (a) that all the elements of a given system are unambiguous, i.e. approaching them in the course of one's life within the system they never change face, they never behave like the following picture (which may look like a young woman but can change into an old woman) and the concepts never experience analogous changes. For if they do, then the 'system' contains the means of blowing itself up, i.e. it is not really a system. This is a very unrealistic assumption; it is not even true of the relation between humans and animals – think of domestication. Of course, it is always possible to freeze aspects and reactions and some groups, radicals on the right and left included, have developed a great talent in this field. They freeze not only traditional ideas and practices which are the results of long and complicated processes of adaptation but also the most superficial creations of the moment, and so imprison themselves and others in narrow, badly lit and badly aired ideological prisons. The relation between such prisons is correctly described by relativism – relativism is a good account of the ideas of people who dislike change and turn difficulties of communication into matters of principle. To

regard statements, emotions, and all utterances of a human life as being 'relative to a system' also assumes (b) that one cannot learn new ways of life. For if one can, then one system is potentially all systems and the restriction 'relative to system A', *while useful for special purposes*, loses its power as a *general characterization of knowledge*. Of course, starting from one presumed 'system' the learning process will have a different structure than when starting from another, but it will tend to lead away from the 'system', as all learning does. Thirdly, different 'forms of life' have a different fate when put in the same surroundings, and some of them fare badly in the eyes of their own practitioners. This shows that there is something like a resistance in the world. But – and with this I come to a very important point which has been emphasized by Niels Bohr – the resistance is much weaker than is assumed by the professional realists of today: a good life in a non-technological society without science but with anthropomorphic gods *is* possible. Ancient Greece, Republican Rome and Rome after Augustus are examples. In Rome the gods even took part in politics. Yet there is no way of ever finding the 'laws of the resistance' for this would mean anticipating the results of all future historical developments. All we can do is to describe the difficulties we have found in the past and under very specific historical conditions, to live with the world as with a friend and to change our habits when life gets bad.

A: But what becomes now of philosophy?

B: Who cares? Special subjects don't interest me. Besides, those people who call themselves philosophers are already attending to the matter.

A: But you are a philosopher yourself!

B: No. I am a professor of philosophy.

A: What's the difference?

B: A philosopher is a free spirit – a professor is a civil servant who has to stick to a schedule but gets paid for it.

A: Don't you find anything redeeming in philosophy?

B: Not in 'philosophy', but in the books or in the tales of some of the people who are now writing in the field – though I admit that I read very little of that stuff. I prefer reading histories, art histories included, the work of physicists, and, of course, crime stories, novels; I also watch TV series such as Dallas and Dynasty. Plato and Aristotle I admire immensely, but they were not 'philosophers' – they dealt with everything.

A: Is that not the real task of philosophy?

B: Well, if you think a philosopher is a universal dilettante who tries to see things in perspective and tries to stop people from forcing others into their beliefs, be it now by arguments or by other means of coercion, then I certainly am a philosopher – but so are journalists and playwrights. But most of the people who call themselves philosophers today want to be 'professionals', i.e. they want to approach things in a special way and in this way secure themselves a place apart from other human activities.

A: Still, you do talk about professional philosophical topics, about rationality ...

B: I talk about these topics not because they are philosophical topics but because they have bad effects – 'rationality' often has been used to enslave people, or even to kill them. Robespierre was a rationalist ...

A: He was a dogmatist, not a critical rationalist ...

B: Are you dreaming? There hardly ever existed a movement so vapid and at the same time so dogmatic as this so called 'critical' rationalism. True, critical rationalists don't kill people, but they kill their minds ...

A: You cannot say that; the idea that science proceeds through falsifications was a real discovery ...

B: It was neither a new discovery – lots of people in antiquity and later mentioned the importance of counter-examples – nor is the statement correct: many important changes in the sciences occurred without any falsification anywhere. Falsification is great as a rule of thumb; it stinks as a condition of scientific rationality ...

A: I am sorry I mentioned critical rationalism. But let me continue: you introduced a new philosophical concept, the concept of incommensurability!

B: Well, I certainly did not mean this to be a positive contribution. What I wanted to do was to criticize a popular but to my mind misguided view on explanation and reduction. To criticize this view I pointed to a feature of scientific change that could not be covered by it and I called the feature 'incommensurability'. As far as I am concerned incommensurability is no difficulty for the sciences or, for that matter, for anyone else – it is a difficulty only for some very naive philosophical theories and, as these theories were regarded as essential ingredients of a certain type of 'rationality', for this type as well. But it was blown up into a profound feature of all 'creative' thought and it was soon used to provide equally profound reasons for the lack of understanding between cultures and scientific schools. That, to me, is just nonsense. Misunderstandings exist. They often occur when people have different customs or speak different languages. The phenomenon I called incommensurability accounts only for a small part of these misunderstandings and I regard it not only as naive but as *downright criminal* to blow it up into One Big Monster that is responsible for all the troubles in science and the world at large. Of course, incommensurability is a boon for philosophers and sociologists – and by this I now mean people who call themselves 'philosophers' or 'sociologists' – who like big words, simple concepts and trite explanations and who love giving the impression they understand the deep reasons behind troublesome affairs. The matter is criminal because it emphasizes difficulties, dwells on them, makes theories about them instead of trying to get out of them. Different cultures now seem to be doomed to talk past each other just as Einstein seemed doomed forever to misunderstand the wonderful discoveries of the quantum theory. Let us agree that Plato is different from Aristotle but let us not forget that Aristotle spent twenty years at the Academy and certainly learned how to talk the Platonic lingo. Let us also remember that Bohr and Einstein liked each other, often talked to each other and that Einstein *accepted* Bohr's way of defusing his counter-examples. No 'incommensurability' here! Of course, he still had a different metaphysics, but that is not a matter of incommensurability except for the most doctrinaire rationalist.

A: Well, that certainly was a long speech. What I get out of it is that while you don't mind tinkering a little here and a little there you have no coherent philosophy.

B: You are right – I don't have a philosophy, if by a philosophy you mean a set of principles and their application, or a basic unchanging attitude. I do have a philosophy in a different sense, I have a world view, but I can't spell it out, it only shows itself when I run into something that conflicts with it; it also changes and it is more an attitude than a theory unless by 'theory' you mean a story whose content is never the same.

A: Now I understand why philosophers don't want to have anything to do with you.

B: And rightly so, for I am not one of them. Most philosophers who talk about relativism talk about Rorty, who chimes in with their conceptions, or about Kuhn, who has a theory and tries hard to appease professional philosophers, or about sociologists such as Bloor who again have theories. And the existentialists already have their heroes – Kierkegaard and Heidegger. Besides, Rorty, Kuhn, Bloor, Heidegger are committed in the sense that they regard themselves as professionals and centre their lives around their 'work'. I am not a professional, I don't want to be, and I rarely 'think philosophy'. I never studied philosophy – I got my first philosophical

job through friends and the intervention of Schrödinger who knew me as a student – and when I read the one or the other philosophical book, I did it because of a passing whim and not because of an overall plan.
A: But people have associated your work with that of Popper, or that of Kuhn.
B: A simple mistake. I knew Popper and his collaborators and I talked with them in their own terms, just as one does in polite society. The talks were published – and now some people think I am a Popperian.
A: Are you?
B: Are you kidding?
A: What about Kuhn? He is a relativist of sorts, you seem to be a relativist; he argues historically, you argue historically – and both of you talk about incommensurability.
B: Yes, I learned a lot from Kuhn. It was he (and Carl Friedrich von Weizsaecker) who convinced me that you have to approach science, the arts etc. etc. historically, by retracing their life stories, and not logically, i.e. by trying to capture some permanent structures. Analogies there are – but no permanent structures. But having learned this from Kuhn I feel rather uneasy about his attempt to reintroduce theories (role of normal science, of revolutions etc.) and with his more recent attempts to try to find a philosophical 'foundation' for these theories. That, I say, replaces fact by fantasy.
A: Now you talk like a positivist.
B: Why not? The positivists made mistakes, but they also had very interesting things to say. At any rate: there is history – and history consists of a great variety of stories – and there is scientific practice which is part of history. That is all. We also found incommensurability in different ways and have different opinions about it. Kuhn found incommensurability in the course of his historical studies, I found it elaborating on the old positivistic debate about basic statements. He regards it as an important feature of scientific change, I regard it as a puff of hot air extinguishing some burnt-down positivistic candles.
A: And relativism?
B: I don't think Kuhn is a relativist, though many people accuse him of being one. I was a relativist, at least in one of the many meanings of this term, but I now regard relativism

as a very useful and, above all, humane approximation to a better view . . .
A: Which view?
B: I haven't found it yet.
A: Now let us get back to the matter of your being a philosopher –
B: . . . yes, this is a major difference between Kuhn and myself. Kuhn aspires to be a philosopher, a professional. That is not my aim, assuming I have aims . . .
A: But you wrote many papers, quite a heap of them – there are two volumes of your collected essays and even they don't contain all the stuff you have written.
B: That was an accident. Twenty to thirty years ago I travelled a lot and I gave many talks. I liked to give talks; I was paid the fare, I met friends, and I could upset people by making silly statements in public. I never prepared my talks – I made a few notes and left the rest to inspiration. However, in many cases my talks were part of a lecture series and so the editors pressured me to write them down. This is how most of my papers originated.
A: And *Against Method*?
B: Well, I already told you: Lakatos suggested that we write a book together and I liked the idea. When I wrote *AM* I said: 'This is the last time I shall write anything; now I want to have peace and quiet, watch TV, lie in the sun, go to the movies, have a few affairs and just make minimal preparations for the lectures that feed me.'
A: But you continued to write.
B: That was the biggest mistake of my life. You know I never expected *AM* to create the furor it did create – it has by now been translated into eighteen languages, Romanian being the last one, Korean is just before the door. There were descriptions, criticisms, attacks in major journals, in *Science*, for example, where they sent a special photographer to get a picture of me with my King-Kong poster in the background, in *The New York Review of Books* and so on. Most of the criticisms I did not know about, for I do not read intellectual journals, some of them were sent to me by friends – and almost all of them were of a an appalling stupidity. I had not encountered this phenomenon before – my earlier discussions occurred in small circles with people I knew very well and who knew me –

I was surprised and made the mistake of being drawn into the debate. That was a waste of time and energy.

A: But now, at last, you will stop writing.

B: Alas, I am not yet that far. I promised my friend – and now beloved wife – Grazia to write a book about 'Reality' . . .

A: REALITY?

B: Yes, reality – this is just a working title. It will deal with problems of the quantum theory, late medieval painting, Roman statuary, Brecht, Stanislavsky – and many other things, and it will deal with these things briefly, on no more than 120 pages. It may take me another ten years – I am not in any hurry – and it will have lots of pictures. Also I am going to write an autobiography.

A: You must think very highly of yourself to write an autobiography!

B: No, no – that is not the reason. Last year, in 1988, Austria celebrated – well you cannot really say 'celebrate' – it commemorated its unification with Germany: fifty years ago Austria became part of the Reich. Many Austrians rejoiced when the event occurred – there was a tremendous outburst of enthusiasm. Now, in 1988, the question was: what to do? Some good and considerate people wanted to make a gesture, they wanted to think about the past in a useful way. They were joined by liars, sycophants, ignoramuses and all sorts of people with special interests – that at least is how the whole matter looked to me from the distance, from the USA or from Switzerland. I watched the festivities on TV and I got quite depressed. There was Waldheim. I cannot stand the guy and I was seriously embarrassed long ago when he became the Secretary-General of the United Nations. 'That creep is an Austrian?' I asked myself. (Remember, I am still an Austrian citizen!). I don't know what he did during the Second World War but I do know that I do not like what he is doing now. There were polished condemnations and lengthy humanitarian arias. Many good people participated, as I said; still, I had the feeling that all I heard were empty slogans and vapid promises. I do have an explanation for the fiasco – humanity simply cannot be expressed through abstractions and slogans are not the right instruments for making restitution. So I thought of a different way of dealing with the event. Many prominent Austrians witnessed the occupation as children and were soldiers in the Second World War. 'Why don't these Austrians report their experiences and their feelings?' I asked myself, 'their feelings as they occurred during the fateful years, not hiding anything. They may have been enthusiastic – why don't they say exactly what they felt and how their attitude changed over the years? A confession, an honest report, no treacly sentiments, no lying self-justification! Ingmar Bergman, in his autobiography, describes how as an exchange student in Germany he started loving Hitler – he says this simply, without explanation, just stating a fact – why can't we do the same?' Well, I am not a prominent Austrian, but my stuff is read by a few people, I was an officer in the German army, so, I said to myself, why don't I start the process by telling my own story. There is a second reason why I find the plan attractive. I don't keep records, I have no files, letters I answer and immediately throw away, I have no memorabilia of my parents and relatives – all I have is my memory. I forgot many things, I confused others, for a while I thought I had been near Kiev during the war – I never was – and so I also intended to revive my memory and to explore my past. This, incidentally, is a much better way of explaining one's 'views', i.e. the special secretions one deposits in books and papers, than an 'intellectual autobiography' that contains ideas only and never mentions when and how one got laid for the first time. Einstein wrote an intellectual autobiography and he emphasized that he would stick to ideas only. In principle this is not at all different from the famous autobiography of Josefine Mutzenbacher which follows the heroine through all her sexual adventures with never so much as a word about the movies she saw or the books she read. It is a caricature. So for all these reasons I intend to write an autobiography and its title will be KILLING TIME, for much of my life, unfortunately, was useless hanging around and waiting. But after that, I promise you, I shall shut up and forever keep my peace.

A: And you think anybody is going to believe you?

B: Just wait!

Postscript

Postscript

Rumour has it that while it is possible to examine ideas or systems of ideas in a loose way, in letters, telephone calls, dinner conversations, the proper form for explaining their shape, their implications and the reasons for their acceptance is an essay or a book. The essay (the book) has a beginning, a middle and an end. There is an exposition, a development and a result. After that the idea (the system) is as clear and as well-defined as a dead butterfly in a collector's box.

But ideas, like butterflies, do not merely exist; they develop, they enter into relations with other ideas and they have effects. The whole history of physics was tied to the assumption, first formulated by Parmenides, that some things remain unaffected by change. The assumption was soon transformed: parity conservation is far removed from the conservation of Being. The end of an essay, or a book, though formulated as if it were an end, is therefore not really an end but a transition point which has received undue weight. Like a classical tragedy it erects barriers where no barriers occur.

Modern historians (of science and of other subjects) have found additional faults. The order of description in a scientific paper has little to do with the order of discovery and some of the individual elements turn out to be chimaeras. This does not mean that the writers are lying. Being forced into a special pattern their memory changes and provides the needed (but fictitious) information.

There exist now areas in which the essay, or the research

paper, and especially the textbook have lost much of their former weight. The reason is that the large number of researchers and the flood of research results has increased the rate of change to such an extent that a paper is often obsolete by the time it is published. The forefront of research is defined by conferences, letters to the editor (cf. the *Physical Review Letters*), fax machines. Papers and textbooks not only lag behind, they cannot even be understood without this occasionally rather shapeless form of discourse.

Philosophers pride themselves on being able to find clear principles behind the most extravagant commotion. The 'world of Greek commonsense' (if there was a single such world) was pretty complicated when Parmenides wrote. This did not prevent him from postulating and even proving that reality was different, simple and conquerable by thought. Modern philosophy, though less confident in this respect, still contains the idea of clear structures behind complex events. Some philosophers (but also sociologists and even poets) approach texts accordingly; they look for ingredients that can be made part of a logically acceptable structure and then use this structure to judge the rest.

The attempt is bound to fail. First, because it has no counterpart in the sciences which are important contributors to knowledge. Secondly, because it has no counterpart in 'life'. Life seems clear enough as long as it is routine i.e. as long as people remain docile, read texts in a standard manner and are not challenged in a fundamental way. The clarity dissolves, strange ideas, perceptions, feelings raise their head when routine breaks down. Historians, poets, film-makers have described such events. One example: Pirandello. Compared with these works the logic-bound essays seem to share the unreality of a Barbara Cartland novel. They are fiction, but fiction of a rather uninspiring kind.

Plato thought that the gulf between ideas and life could be bridged by the dialogue – not by a written dialogue which for him was but a superficial account of past events, but by a real, spoken exchange between people of different background. I agree that a dialogue reveals more than an essay. It can provide arguments. It can show the effect of arguments on outsiders or on experts from a different school, it makes explicit the loose ends which an essay or a book tries to conceal and, most importantly, it can demonstrate the chimaerical nature of what we believe to be the most solid parts of our lives. The disadvantage is that all this is done on paper, not in actions, performed by live people, before our eyes. We are again invited to engage in some antiseptic kind of activity or, to use different words, we are again invited merely to think. Again we are far away from the battles between thought, perception, emotion that really shape our lives, 'pure' knowledge included. The Greeks had an institution that produced the needed confrontations – the drama. Plato rejected the drama and thus made his contribution to the logomania that affects so many parts of our culture.

The dialogues of this book are imperfect in many respects. This is especially true of the second dialogue. It is not really a dialogue but a diatribe directed at a helpless victim. The topics are authenticity (which I ridicule), commitment (which I reject), the vagueness of terms which undermines any commitment and the ignorance of experts. My use of examples from astrology should not be misunderstood. Astrology bores me to tears. However it was attacked by scientists, Nobel Prize winners among them, without arguments, simply by a show of authority and in this respect deserved a defence. Medicine has made some progress since I wrote the dialogue but the effects of Western medicine (if there is a single such system, which I doubt) compared with other medical systems are still unknown. We have anecdotal evidence in limited areas, we don't have an overall view. Thus we can say what Western medicine does; we cannot say that it surpasses all other medical systems. The first dialogue is perhaps the best. It reflects the situation in my seminar in Berkeley; Dr Cole has little to do with me but some of the characters (not identifiable by name) are tributes to some wonderful students I had.

The dialogues are philosophical in a very general and nontechnical sense. They might even be called deconstructionist, though my guide was Nestroy (as read by Karl Kraus), not Derrida. In an interview for the Italian journal *Repubblica* I was asked: 'What do you think of the present developments in Eastern Europe and what does philosophy have to say on these matters?' My answer will perhaps explain my attitude a little better. 'These are two entirely different questions,' I said. 'The first question is directed at a living and more or less adequately thinking human being with feelings, prejudices, stupidities, namely: me. The second question is directed at something that does not exist, an abstract monster, "philosophy". Philosophy is even less of a unit than science. There are philosophical schools who either know little of each other, or they fight and despise each other. Some of these schools, logical empiricism for example, have hardly ever dealt with the problems that now arise; besides, they would not be too happy about the increase of religious feelings that accompanied the developments (in some South American countries religion is in the forefront of the battle for liberation). Others, Hegelians for example, have long arias for describing dramatic events and they no doubt will now start singing these arias – with what effect, nobody knows. Besides, there only rarely exists a close relation between the philosophy of a person and his/her political behaviour. Frege was a sharp thinker in matters of logic and the foundations of mathematics – but the politics that appears in his diaries is of the most primitive kind. And that is just the trouble; events such as those that now occur in Eastern Europe and, less visibly, in other parts of the globe and, more generally, all events involving human beings elude intellectual schemes – each of us is challenged, *individually*, to react and, perhaps, to take a stand. If the person that reacts is humane, loving, unselfish then a knowledge of history, philosophy, politics, even basic physics (Sakharov!) may be useful, for s/he may apply it in a humane manner. I say "may be" – for good people have fallen for rotten philosophies and have explained their actions in a misleading and dangerous way. Czeslaw Milosz is an example, and I discussed him in *Farewell to Reason*. Fang Lizhi, the Chinese astrophysicist and dissident, is another. He tries to justify his fight for freedom by reference to universal rights which "disregard race, language, religion and other beliefs". The physical universe, he says, obeys a "cosmological principle" – every place and direction in it is equivalent to every other place and direction; the same, he says, should apply to the moral universe. This is the old universalizing tendency all over again and we see here very clearly where it leads. For if we "disregard" the racial features of a face, if we don't care for the rhythm of the sounds that emerge from its mouth, if we subtract the special and culturally determined gestures that accompany speaking then we have no longer a living human being, we have a monster and such a monster is dead, not free. Besides, what has the physical universe got to do with morality? Assume with the Gnostics that it is a prison, should we then adapt our morals to its prisonlike properties? True, Gnosticism is not popular today – but more recent discoveries indicate that the "cosmological principle", too, may soon be a matter of the past. Should we change our morals when that happens? Only rarely does a sensible philosophy meet a sensible person who then uses it in a humane manner. Vaclav Havel is an example and he shows very clearly that it is not "philosophy" that is challenged by the development, but each individual person. For, to repeat, "philosophy" as a well-defined and homogeneous domain of activity exists as little as does "science". There are the words, there are even concepts, but human existence shows no trace of the boundaries the concepts imply.'